# Helps for

**For Believer**

**Direction in their Walk of Faith.**

## With Study Guide

## James Olah

Book two of the "**Basic Christianity**" series

## June, 2012

# Helps for Young Christians

## For Believers who need Guidance and Direction in their Walk of Faith

A book of handy facts to help you understand the Christian faith,
How to live it, share it and defend it.

Book two of the "Basic Christianity" series
With Study Guide

By: James Olah

©June 2012 James Olah
All Rights Reserved
First Edition June 2012
Revised October 2012
Revised Dec 2012
120 Pages 47,000 Words

**ISBN-13:978-1494399603**
**ISBN-10:1494399601**

Copyrighted Material All rights reserved. No part of this book may be reproduced in any form without permission in writing from the author, except in the case of brief quotations embodied in critical articles or reviews

Copyrighted Material
Please acknowledge all quotes.
Direct permission requests to:
Jso46@hotmail.com

Unless otherwise stated Scripture quotes are taken from the World English Bible, (WEB) and is in the public Domain. It is part of the Online Bible and can be found at: http://www.onlinebible.net/ © 2008

Scripture taken from: The Holy Bible, 21st Century King James Version (KJ21), Copyright 1994, Deuel Enterprises, Inc., Gary, SD 57237, and used by permission. 21st Century King James Version. It is part of the Online Bible and can be found at: http://www.onlinebible.net/

SOJO Books

# Introduction
## Helps for Young Christians

When I became a chaplain for hospice I was required to go through training to prepare me for my new position. I learned what hospice was about, how the rules regulated what we could talk about, how to keep safe when dealing with people with a contagious disease, what I could and couldn't do in a home and a lot of other details. The training took a few weeks interspersed with calls with other staff members so I would understand how the other disciplines worked, and also how each of the chaplains did their work. It was a good combination of training and experience.

Training helped prepare me to do a proper and informed job, and I benefitted from what I learned. Training with experienced staff cuts the learning curve down, so one can come up to speed more quickly and avoid some of the pitfalls of the learning process.

Young Christians need a plan of growth to live the Christian life. That process includes learning how to relate to others, and how to stand for as well as defend their faith. Once you become a Christian your next focus should be learning how to live as a Christian. In order to accomplish that, Christians need to know how to intentionally develop a pattern of actions that develop growth in their faith, maintain a relationship with God and sustain meaningful relationships with others. Understanding who they are in this new relationship with God, and that they are part of a new family, God's family gives them direction. It is essential to learn how to overcome sin and learn how to serve. The ultimate reality for the Christian is the joy of learning to live with "other-world" values and motivation in the current world.

This book is designed to help give an overview of essential components of understanding for living out the Christian life. Along with the brief teaching on specific areas, there are also recommendations of books, websites and podcasts that can help you become even more proficient in that area of your Christian life.

This is not intended to be an exhaustive resource on the topic of Christian growth, but one designed to give you ideas and an overview to help you develop a plan for maturing as a Christian. It is my prayer that this book will give you understanding in specific areas of what you need to learn and how you can grow in your journey of faith.

Pastor Jim Olah

# Table of Contents

# "Helps for Young Christians"
## A learning guide to help you grow in your faith
### Introduction

If you are a new or young Christian then basic information is essential to help you grow and think through your faith. This book is a compilation of articles and handouts I put together to help Christians over the years when I did studies on various topics. Think of this book as a roadmap for Christian growth.

Some people will shrink away from doing some of the things presented in this book. But the fact of the matter is it takes work to grow as a Christian. People will pay good money to go to college, and they will work hard to learn a profession. But the education given these days teaches how to make a living, but seldom does it really teach a person how to live to honor God. You want to earn a good living so you can reap greater benefits and rewards in life. Such studies, as I present here, will also give you rewards in your relationship and walk with God and people and help you live in such a way that you will have rewards in heaven. God offers you a variety of rewards, also called crowns, because of different aspects of faithful living. Do you want God to honor and recognize your faithfulness one day? I do, and I want to point you in the right direction.

It is important to learn as much as you can about your faith. That includes knowing *what* you believe as well as *why* you believe what you do. You need a basis for making decisions and setting spiritual direction that will help you advance in your faith. If the only basis for choosing an action is because "my church or pastor" told me this is what to do, then you are ill equipped to face the difficult issues of life. If a professor at a university sounds smarter than your pastor, then do you choose his or her way? You need to know from a personal understanding of the Bible and a genuine walk with God why you believe what you do and why you stand for what you do as a Christian.

Knowing what you believe and why also helps you to stand up for your faith. When you get a better perception of your faith it will drive you to more serious digging on your own and that helps you improve your understanding. Consider carefully the following scriptures about God's call for you to grow in your faith.

*"Yes, and for this very cause **adding on your part all diligence**, in your faith supply moral excellence; and in moral excellence, knowledge; and in knowledge, self-control; and in self-control patience; and in patience godliness; and in godliness brotherly affection; and in brotherly affection, love. For if these things are yours and abound, they make you to be not idle nor unfruitful to the knowledge of our Lord Jesus Christ. For he who lacks these things is blind, seeing only what is near, having*

*forgotten the cleansing from his old sins. Therefore, brothers, be more diligent to make your calling and election sure. For if you do these things, you will never stumble."* 2 Peter 1:5-10

*"But you, man of God, flee these things, and follow after righteousness, godliness, faith, love, patience, and gentleness. Fight the good fight of faith. Lay hold of the eternal life to which you were called, and you confessed the good confession in the sight of many witnesses. 17 Charge those who are rich in this present world that they not be haughty, nor have their hope set on the uncertainty of riches, but on the living God, who richly provides us with everything to enjoy..."* 1 Timothy 6:11-12

*"...that they do good, that they be rich in good works, that they be ready to distribute, willing to communicate; laying up in store for themselves a good foundation against the time to come, that they may lay hold of eternal life."* 1 Timothy 6:18-19

Paul is calling his readers to *"Lay hold of eternal life"*. This is a command telling believers to take what has been given to us and make it ours. The question is this, "what does it mean to take hold of eternal life if one is already saved?" If one is saved they already have eternal life. So what does it mean to take hold of eternal life?

Let me illustrate it in this way. Suppose that you inherited 5,000 acres of fertile farm land. This land is very valuable. It has rich soil, it is well drained and has an effective irrigation system, and thus it has the potential to make lots of money. With the inheritance came all the equipment needed to farm the land. However, you have never farmed and you don't know what to do. You don't know what crops to plant; and you don't know how to run the machinery. Some of the tractors and harvesters are so large they intimidate you. You can't do this alone. You need planting advice, when to plant those crops, how to plant them, how to harvest each type, and where to sell it. You need someone to show you how to use the equipment and maintain it. You feel absolutely overwhelmed, but you want to take on the challenge.

As you contemplate this do you think you are going to make mistakes? Do you think you will do some things wrong along the way? Do you think you might even damage the equipment while you are inexperienced? What do you think will help you? It is getting in there and doing it. Learning how to prepare the soil, plant, harvest and sell the product. You have to work on doing something every day and the more experience you get the more your skill level will improve until farming becomes second nature in what you are doing.

To lay hold of eternal life is similar to the above illustration. You have been given a life rich with resources from God. See chapter 13 that describe the resources each Christian has been given by God. God doesn't want you to just posses these qualities; He wants you to use these by putting them into practice in everyday life. To lay hold of eternal life means that you learn how to develop and use your gifts, talents and abilities to serve the Lord. You give your heart to God and learn to love Him and take His message to the world. To lay hold of eternal life is to understand God's resources so you can implement them in your life. When your faith is attacked you need to seek refuge in God and stand strong for your faith. When God gives you material resources use them to serve Him and help others. When you face difficulties in life learn how to trust in God's love and believe that He really does have a plan for you. Using these resources will require you to become proficient in your faith. Here are some examples.

1.  *It means you need to know what you believe.*
2.  *It means you need to learn how to mine the resources found in the depths of God's word.*
3.  *It means you learn the issues of the day so you can expose error and stand for the truth as well as stand against those who hate and oppose God and His ways.*
4.  *It means you learn how to maintain your faith so that you deal with sin and learn how to make your weak areas strong and to stand strong in the midst of trials.*
5.  *It means you learn how to express your faith in your daily life at home, school or work and in your neighborhood.*
6.  *It means you learn how to discern the error in the world and the deceptive ways of Satan.*
7.  *It means that you learn how God has gifted you and you use that to serve others and strengthen the church.*
8.  *It means that you learn what the faith walk is, for the just shall live by faith.*

Paul expresses this thought in Philippians 2:12, *"So then, my beloved, even as you have always obeyed, not only in my presence, but now much more in my absence, work out your own salvation with fear and trembling."* Notice he does not say work for your salvation; you cannot earn your salvation by works. This salvation you received by faith, is to be worked out, to be expressed, to be lived in daily life. Many want the Christian life to be automatic and requiring no effort on our part to bring us to maturity, but it takes work and commitment to develop the kind of godly life God has called all believers to express and experience.

The Writer of Hebrews reinforces this teaching that we need to take responsibility for the direction of our life. You have to decide if you want to be a *milk-Christian* or a *meat-Christian*. That means you choose between being Peter Pan who wants to remain a child or like the Apostle Paul who demonstrated the maturity God wants to see developed in each of us. Read the following passage every day for a week and ask yourself which kind of Christian you want to be. To be a meat-Christian demands work and dedication on your behalf and that is what I want to help you accomplish through this book. It also takes time to develop.

> *"About him we have many words to say and hard to interpret, seeing you have become dull of hearing. For although by this time you should be teachers, you again need to have someone teach you the rudiments of the first principles of the oracles of God. You have come to need milk, and not solid food. For everyone who lives on milk is not experienced in the word of righteousness, for he is a baby. But solid food is for those who are full grown,* **who by reason of use** *have their senses exercised to discern good and evil. Therefore leaving the teaching of the first principles of Christ, let us press on to perfection\*—not laying again a foundation of repentance from dead works, of faith toward God, of the teaching of baptisms, of laying on of hands, of resurrection of the dead, and of eternal judgment. This will we do, if God permits."* Hebrews 5:11-6:3 (\*maturity)

This book is designed to give you instruction about the specific areas of your faith you should seek to develop. The result is that you will grow in your faith and become a "meat-Christian" who knows how to feed himself and take care of his own needs. That is what is called growing up in your faith. Do you want to become a mature Christian who knows how to see and address the needs that face him in daily life? Along with the Bible this is a handy guide to help you in this journey.

Again, I remind you that this book is not a "make you feel good" kind of book. It is a work book that points you in the right direction. It requires work to learn these truths and apply them to your life. It may overwhelm you at first, but the more you work on each area of this book the greater insight you will gain into living the Christian life. Your work will help you discover that you are gaining a working knowledge of your faith and with it come joy, confidence and the ability to better walk in God's way. I pray that your journey may be productive and fruitful as the exercises draw you closer to our great God and Savior.

# Chapter 1 - Become familiar with basic doctrines of the faith

Each believer should know the central truths of the faith. Basic beliefs that conservative Bible believing Christians hold in common are called *The Fundamentals*. This is actually where the term fundamentalist had its beginning. The term did not refer to extremist but basic beliefs of the faith.

Five Fundamentals had to be believed if a church wanted to be considered a bible- believing Church. Churches that didn't subscribe to these teachings were considered liberal. What are the five fundamentals a church or Christian needed to believe?

1. The deity of our Lord Jesus Christ (John 1:1, 5:18, 20:28; Hebrews 1:8-9)
2. The virgin birth of Christ (Isaiah 7:14; Matthew 1:23; Luke 1:27)
3. The blood atonement (Acts 20:28; Romans 3:25, 5:9; Ephesians 1:7; Hebrews 9:12-14)
4. The bodily resurrection (Luke 24:36-46; 1 Corinthians 15:1-4, 15:14-15)
5. The inerrancy of the scriptures themselves (Rom. 15:4; 2 Timothy 3:16-17; 2 Peter 1:20)

Most bible-believing churches have a very similar list of doctrinal beliefs. Some go into much more detail, and also add other doctrines. Below is an abbreviated list of basic biblical beliefs. This statement is from the church I was serving when I wrote this paper. Make sure you check out the doctrinal beliefs of your church or the church you choose to attend. Know what you believe. When you know truth, this protects you from both false teaching and from being deceived by errant worldviews.

Many people say, "Why don't we just put doctrine aside and all get along?" Our doctrine defines who we are and is, therefore, very important. Doctrine is the basis of how we establish our faith and how we understand God. Doctrine defines what life is about.

The Bible often warns believers to be aware of false teachers who will subvert the truth and seek to take you away from the truth. If any teaching does not line up with the truth of scripture, then it is false doctrine and must be avoided. The cults have doctrinal statements, but some have other sources of authority than the Bible. They claim to believe in the deity of Christ, but they deny some essential aspect of His person and work. Some claim salvation by faith, but they require works to finish off the salvation process. Some add to the doctrine of eternal punishment and claim purgatory as a means of paying for one's sins. Many others flat out deny the existence of hell. It is very important to know Bible doctrine, for by it you know the parameters of your faith.

Don't be afraid of the word doctrine for it simply means the organization of the various teachings of the Bible that express its truth in a succinct manner. Theology books are simply extensive explanations of biblical doctrines. Some free Bible programs for your computer or tablet offer theology books as add-ons. <u>Moody Handbook of Theology</u> by Paul Enns is a popular Theology book, and he does a good job of presenting the various views. Charles Ryrie has also written <u>Basic Theology: A Popular Systematic Guide to Understanding Biblical Truth</u>.

The first doctrine listed below is given in extensive form. This is an illustration of how much depth some statements are for churches and Christian organizations. Some will go into even more detail than that because they want it clearly spelled out. I present this first doctrine in an extensive style to accommodate one of the questions in the study guide. We need a good grasp on the basis of our authority for making all decisions and for establishing the essential beliefs of our faith. Read through the following doctrinal list to gain a better understanding of how biblical beliefs are expressed. Such doctrines are extrapolated from reading and studying the Bible. They are not long, but I want you to get a grasp the church's basic beliefs.

A. The Bible, consisting of all the books of the Old and New Testaments, is the Word of God, a supernaturally given revelation from God Himself, concerning Himself, His being, nature, character, will and purposes; and concerning man, his nature, need and duty and destiny. We believe that "all Scripture is given by inspiration of God," by which we understand the whole Bible is inspired in the sense that holy men of God "were moved by the Holy Spirit" to write the very words of Scripture. We believe that this divine inspiration extends equally and fully to all parts of the writings—historical, poetical, doctrinal, and prophetical—as appeared in the original manuscripts. We believe that the whole Bible in the originals is therefore without error. We believe that all the Scriptures center about the Lord Jesus Christ in His person and work in His first and second coming, and hence that no portion, even of the Old Testament, is properly read, or understood, until it leads to Him. We also believe that all the Scriptures were designed for our practical instruction (Mark 12:26, 36; 13:11; Luke 24:27, 44; John 5:39; Acts 1:16; 17:2–3; 18:28; 26:22–23; 28:23; Rom. 15:4; 1 Cor. 2:13; 10:11; 2 Tim. 3:16; 2 Pet. 1:21). (Check out audio messages by Dr. McRae "The Christian and His Bible") - http://www.gbfc-tx.org/Pages/BillMcrae.html

B. We believe in the Triune God, eternally existing in three persons: Father, Son and Holy Spirit, co-eternal in being, co-identical in nature, co-equal in power and glory, and having the same attributes and perfections. (Deut. 6:4; Matthew 28:19; 2 Cor. 13:14)

C. Jesus is the Eternal Son of God who became man without ceasing to be God. He committed no sin as man, and while on earth revealed God to us. (John 1:1-2, 14, 18; Luke 1:35; Philippians 2:5-8)

Jesus accomplished our redemption through His death on the cross and His literal resurrection from the dead. (Isaiah 53:4-6; Romans 3:24-25; I Corinthians 15:17-20; Ephesians 1:7; I Peter 2:24)

D. The Holy Spirit is a Divine person who convicts the world of sin, of righteousness, and of judgment; and that He is the supernatural agent in regeneration, baptizing all believers into the body of Christ, indwelling and sealing them unto the day of redemption. (John 16:8-11; 1 Corinthians 12:12-14; 2 Cor. 3:6; Romans 8:9; Ephesians 1:13-14, 4:30)

E. Man was created in the image and likeness of God, but in Adam's sin the race fell, inherited a sinful nature, and became alienated from God: and, that man is totally depraved, and of himself, utterly unable to remedy his lost condition. (Genesis 1:26-27; Romans 3:10-23, 5:12; Ephesians 2:1-3 & 12)

F. Salvation is the gift of God brought to man by grace and received by personal faith in the Lord Jesus Christ, whose precious blood was shed on Calvary for the forgiveness of sin. (John 3:16, 5:24, 14:6; Romans 10:9-13; Ephesians 1:7, 2:8-9)

G. All who are truly redeemed are kept by the power of God and are thus secure in Christ forever. (John 3:16; 5:24; 10:27-30; Romans 8:1, 38-39; Ephesians 4:30) (Some fundamental churches disagree on this point. Some believe you can lose your salvation once saved and some don't believe you can lose your salvation once you are truly saved.)

H. Every believer possesses two natures, with provision made for victory of the new nature over the old nature through the power of the indwelling Holy Spirit. (Romans 6:13; 8:12-13; Galatians 5:16-25; Ephesians 4:22-24)

I. All believers are called to live a life separated from the world and in such a manner so as not to bring reproach unto their Savior and Lord. (Romans 12:1-2; 2 Corinthians 6:14-7:1; 1 Thessalonians 4:3-7; I John 2:15-17)

J. The True Church is a spiritual organism made up of all born-again persons, Christ, Himself, is the head of the Church. (I Corinthians 12:12-

14; Ephesians 1:22-23; 4:1-6; 5:22-27) Provision for the establishment and continuance of local churches is clearly taught and defined in the New Testament. (Acts 14:27; 20:17, 28-32; I Timothy 3:1-13; Titus 1:5-11, I Peter 5:1-4)

K. Angels are spiritual beings who were created sinless. Some fell and became demons. Those that did not fall continued on to serve God. Satan is the head of the demons. (Isaiah 14:12-14; Ezekiel 28:11-19; Genesis 3:1-19; Romans 5:12-14; Colossians 2:15; Revelations 12:1-9)

L. We believe in the bodily resurrection of all men, the saved to eternal life with God in heaven, and the unsaved to judgment and everlasting punishment in the lake of fire. (Matthew 25:41-46; Luke 16:19-31; John 5:28-29, 11:25-26, 14:1-6; Rev. 20:5-6, 11-15)

M. Jesus is going to return to take His saints out of the world as well as to rule the world. We believe in "Blessed Hope", the personal, imminent, pre-tribulation and Pre-millennial coming of the Lord Jesus Christ for His redeemed ones. (1 Thessalonians 4:13-18)

JSO-2/92

# Chapter 2 - SHARING YOUR FAITH

God has called every believer to be his witness. *"But you will receive power when the Holy Spirit has come upon you. You will be witnesses..."* Acts 1:8a. Just as a civilization needs babies to grow, so the church needs converts to in order to grow. Many churches depend on transfers from other churches rather than converts to fill their pews. They have lost sight of God's purpose to reach a lost world.

God wants you to do more than enjoy your own salvation; He wants you to share your faith with those who don't have a sure hope after death. There was lady I led to the Lord in my church. Over the next several months she brought both of her sons to me when they were ready to get saved and I led them to the Lord. Later when I taught an evangelism class that she attended she made an interesting statement. She said, "You mean I could have led my children to the Lord. It's that easy." Yes, you can lead a person to the Lord and they will become God's child and go to heaven and miss hell. Does that interest your?

What information do you need to know in order to share your faith, so a person can make an informed decision to trust Christ as their Savior? What does a person have to know to be saved (to become a child of God, to go to heaven, to be forgiven, to be right with God, to be reconciled to God)?

Below are the truths with which you should become familiar to effectively share the good news of Christ to those who are separated from God. *(See author's Kindle Book: Town of Salvation for a more detailed explanation of salvation. It is the first book in the Basics of Christianity series)* The Bible uses terms for the unsaved such as lost, enemies of God, unbelievers, those without hope and aliens from the commonwealth of God.

**Here are the essential truths a person should believe to be saved.**

A. *Everyone is a sinner.* (Romans 3:23) Sin is a violation of God's Law in any way. We only have to break one of God's laws to be a law breaker. (James 2:10) Sin is not just doing wrong; it is also not doing right. (James 4:17) Because all have sinned, all are in need of salvation. (John 3:18, 36) It only took one sin to make Adam and Eve sinners in need of redemption.

B. *God is Holy,* (Habakkuk 1:13; 1 Peter 1:16) therefore He cannot tolerate sin, and must punish it. (Ezekiel 18:4, Romans 3:23)

C. The *penalty for sin* is eternal separation from God eternal punishment in the lake of fire. (Matthew 25:41-46; Revelation 20:11-14, 21:8)

D. *Jesus was eternal God and perfect man.* Because he was perfect man, he could pay the penalty for a sinner with His death, but because He was God He could pay the penalty of sin for all of mankind. (1 Peter 2:22-24; Philippians 2:5-8; Romans 3:24-25; 5:6-10)

E. God offers salvation to all who come to Him by faith. (John 1:12, 3:16, 5:24, 6:47; Romans 10:9-13)

F. One must personally accept the salvation Christ provided through his redemptive work on the cross. (1 John 5:11-13. Romans 5:6-8, 10:9-10, 13; John 5:24)

G. One must come to God by faith. What is faith? There are three parts to saving faith. (Romans 5:1; Ephesians 2:8-9)

   1. *KNOWLEDGE*: One must know the truth of the gospel. That truth is: *"Man is a sinner, man is incapable to remedy his sinful condition, and he is under penalty for his sin. Jesus, the infinite God/man paid the penalty for sin by his death on the cross, and He offers us salvation as a gift we receive by faith."*

   2. *BELIEF*: One must go a step further beyond knowledge. Many know the truth about their condition and the purpose of the death of Christ, but they don't believe that it was for them. We must believe the facts of the gospel to be true. We believe it by personalizing it. Such belief looks like this: *"I am a sinner; I can't make myself acceptable, I deserve hell because of my sin. Jesus' death made complete payment for my sin. I need to accept the gift of salvation by faith. I have personalized the truth and believe it to be true and it applies to me."*

   3. *TRUST*: It is not enough to believe that Jesus died for one's sins, but that faith must be expressed in trust. "*I know Jesus provided redemption, I now place my trust for salvation, eternal life, forgiveness, eternity and reconciliation with God in the finished work of Jesus Christ alone so I can gain an eternal relationship with God.*"

   People may say they believe a plane will fly and can carry them to their destination, but if they don't get into the plane then they do not trust it to take them anywhere. Your belief in Christ as Savior must be expressed by placing your trust in Jesus Christ alone to save you from the penalty of your sin. As in the plane illustration, you must get onboard.

Romans 10:9-13 talks about the act of placing your trust in Christ. You believe in your heart, and you proclaim your trust in Christ by calling on God to save you. Faith in your heart needs to be expressed:

*"That if you will **confess with your mouth** that Jesus is Lord, and **believe in your heart** that God raised him from the dead, you will be saved. For **with the heart, one believes unto righteousness; and with the mouth confession is made unto salvation. For, "Whoever will call on the name of the Lord will be saved."** Romans 10:9-10, 13 (Emphasis added.)*

Just remember that salvation is not accomplished by reciting a formula of saying certain words and you're in. It is entering into a relationship with God. This comes from a heartfelt recognition of the truth and a sincere desire to know God and become right with Him. It is the establishment of a lifelong friendship. Such a prayer of calling on the name of the Lord and expressing your faith for salvation could be articulated in this way:

*"Dear God, I know that you are a holy God and I have offended you by my sin. (This would be a good place to acknowledge how you have specifically failed God.) I believe with all my heart that Jesus died and paid my sin's penalty on the cross so I would not have to pay for my sin in hell for eternity. I now place my trust in Jesus Christ by asking Him to be my Savior and to take away my sins so I can be acceptable to You and enter Your heaven when I die. Lord, I want to get to know you and become best friends. Thank you for saving me and accepting me. In Jesus's name I pray. Amen."*

It is not enough to just know what salvation is, but God calls us to share that message with the lost. Many churches are dying today because they are not taking this responsibility seriously.

One of the books I recommend below is **Got Style.** The reason I like this book is because it describes how God uses the different personalities of people to reach non-believers. There is not just one way to share the gospel and reach the lost. When you understand your style you can be more confident in sharing Christ in a way that is comfortable for the way God has gifted you. Read the reviews and listen to the podcast. One review described the various styles of evangelism. The evangelism styles described (with one characteristics of each style) are:

1. *Assertive* (confident)
2. *Analytical* (logical -Apologetics)
3. *Story-telling* (engaging)
4. *Relational* (conversational)

5. *Invitational* (hospitable)
6. *Incarnational* (compassionate)

http://www.evangelismcoach.org/2009/personality-based-evangelism/ There is also a podcast that can give you more information. Another review of the book that gives more information of each can be found at: http://www.lifeandleadership.com/book-summaries/johnson-got-style.html Take the test to discover your evangelism style. Then read up on the various styles. http://www.repentandturn.com/EvangelismStylesQuiz.html

Recommended resources:
- **Evangelism Explosion** by D. James Kennedy.
- **Got Style?** Personality-based evangelism by Jeffrey A. Johnson. Published by Judson Press. This is an important book for it presents 7 different styles of evangelism. Helps you to learn your most effective style of evangelism.
- Resource sites: http://www.goodseed.com/
- Training: http://evangelismexplosion.org/ministries/

*JSO-7/92*

# Chapter 3 - FUTURE OF YOUR FAITH

The Bible is unique in that it speaks of the future in very accurate ways. As much as one third of the Bible is prophecy. Because so much of it has already been fulfilled we can have strong confidence that what has not been fulfilled will be at the appropriate time. Here are some terms that are used in talking about prophecy. These speak of events yet to come.

A. *LAST DAYS*: The Bible speaks of the Last Days which describe a time before and during the Tribulation and His Return.(2 Timothy 3:1-7, 4:2-4)

B. *RAPTURE*: This is an event when Jesus returns in the clouds and takes all the believers (his children) out of this world. Even though the word rapture is not found in the Bible, the teaching of it is clear. (I Corinthians 15:51-53; I Thessalonians 1:9, 4:13-18. Titus 2:12-13; James 5:7-8; I John 3:2-3)

C. *PRE-TRIBULATION RAPTURE*: I believe in a pre-tribulation rapture of the church. That means that Jesus comes to take all the believers out of the world before the seven years of tribulation as described in Revelation 6-19. Some believe in a *mid-tribulation rapture, a pre-wrath rapture and a post-tribulation rapture*. Why do I believe in a Pre-tribulation view of the rapture? For further explanation beyond what is presented here, see: http://bible.org/question/what-are-top-three-reasons-you-believe-pre-trib-rapture

1.  *Nature of the Tribulation*. It is Jewish in nature. (Jeremiah 30:7) It is the time of "Jacob's (Israel's) Trouble." (Daniel 9:24-27) It is a time God has determined upon "Daniel's people".

2.  *The teaching of imminence*. Such passages as I Thessalonians 5:6; Titus 2:13; Revelation 3:3 all warn the believer to be watching for the Lord Himself, not for signs that would precede His coming. Once the tribulation starts we know exactly when the second coming will happen. (Rapture and second coming are two distinct events separated by seven years.)

3.  *The church is not a recipient of God's wrath*. The tribulation is a time when God will pour out His wrath upon the world. (Rev. 3:10, 1 Thessalonians 1:10, 5:9) Yes, the church faces tribulation

in the world, but not God's wrath. The Tribulation is a specific time of God's wrath on the world. (Rev. 6:17)

4.  *Structure of the book of Revelation.* In the structure of Revelation the Church is seen in Revelation 1-3, but when the Tribulation is described in Revelation 4-19 the Church is not mentioned on earth in these chapters. In chapter 20 the Tribulation ends and the Kingdom age begins.

5.  *Tribulation will be a time of judgment for Gentiles.* (Rev. 3:10) "Those who dwell on the earth" is a phrase in Revelation that describes the unsaved.

D.  *LENGTH OF TRIBULATION* will be **7** years in duration. Dan. 9:24-27 indicates it will be the 70th "7". Half of the tribulation is indicated as 1260 days (3 1/2 years). (Revelation 11:3, 12:6)

E.  *ANTICHRIST* will be established by his mark, (666). (Revelation 13; 2, 16-18; 2 Thessalonians 2:3-8, Daniel 7) He will rule over all the nations, establish a world-wide religion, and control the world economics.

F.  *RAPTURED BELIEVERS WILL BE JUDGED* after the rapture and given rewards for their faithfulness. They will also receive their new bodies and rewards at this time. (1 Corinthians 3:11-15; 15:51-53; 2 Corinthians 5:9-10; Revelation 22:12)

Recognizing that you will be rewarded for your faithfulness is a very important incentive God wants you to appreciate. Understanding your rewards is important, for God reveals this to motivate you to faithfulness. We don't understand all the implications of these crowns now, but you can imagine if God has designed them, they will not be insignificant in any way, nor will they be as worthless as the trophies we win here on earth. I'm adding this little explanation below to help you understand what you have to do to win one of these crowns come Judgment Day.

What Crown do you want to win by your actions?

There are five crowns (and maybe more) that are available for you to win through your faithful living. One does not have to be a pastor or missionary to win these crowns, you only need to be faithful in living the Christian life by obeying God's word and applying His word to your situations in life. Can you imagine that after God saved us that he even rewards us for living in the way He empowered us to live in salvation? That is the expression of a God who loves us and delights in doing good things for us.

Here are the five crowns available for you to win based on your faithfulness in specific areas.

*Imperishable Crown.* (1 Corinthians 9:24-25)This is the crown given to those who run the race of life and "exercise self-control in all things," Doing what you know is right in spite of how you feel or how strong your sinful urges are. You remain committed to doing what God calls us to do. Paul is calling you to be a person of character who works hard for the cause of the faith.

*Crown of Joy.* (Philippians 4:1, 1 Thessalonians 2:19-20) This crown is for those who share the gospel and lead people to Christ. These who share the gospel with the lost receive the crown of Joy.

*Crown of Righteousness.* (2 Timothy 4:7-8) This crown is reserved for those who, like Paul, have lived for Christ's return and can say, "I have fought a good fight, I have finished the course, I have kept the faith." Do you get tired of running the race, whether it be serving the Lord in Church, or just living by the authority of the Word of God? God calls us to be faithful, even when we feel like giving up or that we are the only one doing all the work. Remember, we are faithfully serving because we want to please God, not to seek our own glory. So what if others are not faithful? God will not judge you for how they failed but for how you were faithful. We aren't faithful because we are in a competition with other believers, but because we love God.

*Crown of Life.* (James 1:12) When we are faithful in living the Christian life and seeking to honor God through our trials and difficulties in life we will find that God plans to reward such faithfulness. This crown is for the man or woman who "perseveres under trial". That means you remain faithful for the Lord. If a person offends you or hurts you, does that mean you should forsake the Lord and give up serving Him? Are you going to let their sinful actions dictate your actions or cause you to sin? Are you going to allow them to steal your crown and joy? This means that you are to persevere in spite of what others say and do. Decide to intentionally be faithful to the Lord as you work your way through your trials, sufferings and losses.

*Crown of Glory.* (1 Peter 5:1-4) This one is for the faithful shepherd or pastor who watches over God's flock. This is given to pastors who "shepherd" the flock of God willingly, sacrificially, humbly and with integrity. It is being found faithful in the responsibility and opportunity God has given you, and caring for God's people in an overseeing way.

Learn more about this judgment and crowns at the following sites
http://www.gotquestions.org/heavenly-crowns.html
http://bible.org/article/doctrine-rewards-judgment-seat-bema-christ

G. The tribulation period will end with the *Battle of Armageddon* when Antichrist gathers the nations at Jerusalem to destroy the Jews. Christ returns, defeats and destroys the enemies of His people. (Zechariah 14:1-15, Revelation 19:11-21)

H. Satan will be bound 1000 years while Christ reigns on the earth. (Revelation 20:1-6)

I. Israel and the nations will be judged. (Matthew 25:31-46)

J. *The thousand year reign of Christ* will be characterized by peace, justice, prosperity, joy, and righteousness. No longer will man be able to blame their environment for their sinful condition. (Revelation 20:4-6, Zechariah 14:16-21; Isaiah 11:1-9, 12:3-4; Amos 9:13; Isaiah 30:23-25; 35:3-6, 30:26, 60:22; Psalm 72:7)

K. The thousand year kingdom reign of Christ on earth ends with a battle with Satan. (Revelation 20:7-10)

L. *White throne judgment* will focus on all unsaved people from all ages. (Revelation 20:11-15) People in Hell will suffer forever and never enjoy the love or fellowship of God again. (Luke 16:19-31, Rev. 14:9-12, 20:14-15; 21:8; 22:11, 14-15)

M. Those that go to heaven will enjoy God's presence, and will experience eternal blessing and joy and will serve God. (Psalm 16:11; John 14:1-4; Revelation 7:15-17; 21:1-27; 22:1-5)

JSO-7/92

# Chapter 4 - GROWTH IN YOUR FAITH

What will help a person advance in their faith as well as in their understanding of God? Salvation is not just a ticket into heaven, but it is an enablement of a new life so we can live differently on earth in a way that will please God. Christianity is the reconciliation of our relationship with God, so the main purpose of salvation is getting to know God and spending time with Him. Jesus describes eternal life in John 17:3 as knowing God and Jesus Christ.

How does one grow in their faith and relationship with God? Take the time to look at the scriptures that go with each of the topics. (Holy Bible means Holy book. It is also called the Word of God. Holy Scriptures means holy writings. What do those numbers mean? John 17:3 means it is the gospel of John and we find the 17th chapter and the 3rd verse.)

A. *Study the Bible.* Get to know what you believe, and what it is that God has in store for you. The Bible reveals God. As you get to know what He is like you can then approach Him in truth. The Bible is your road map to your new life in Christ. It teaches you the Christian way, the way God works in and through people's lives. The Bible is God's truth to help us understand Him properly so we can draw close to Him in truth. Seek to avoid looking at Bible study as simply a duty to God, but as your opportunity to read a love letter He has sent you telling you many exciting and wonderful truths to help you experience the Spirit-led life. (Hosea 4:6, Matthew 4:4; Acts 20:32, 1 Peter 2:2; Hebrews 5:13-14; Deuteronomy 32:46-47, Colossians. 3:16)

B. *Develop a Prayer Life.* Learn how to pray biblically. Prayer is talking to your heavenly Father as a friend. Prayer is asking for help and provision for your needs in life because God is interested in being involved in your life. Intercession prayer is praying for the needs of others. Confession of sin is acknowledges your sin to God and is essential in your prayer life because it clears the way to have open communication with God. Praise is recognize God's greatness and then taking the time to exalt Him, His greatness and His involvement in our life. Thanksgiving is recognition of the things he has done in your life as well as in others. Your faith should be expressed in a manner that shows absolute confidence in this all powerful God. Don't be afraid to ask for big things. Always seek to express how your request will fulfill some aspect of the will of God for your life or others. (Luke 18:1; Matthew 7:7-11; John 14:13, 16:23-24; I John 3:22-23, 5:14-15, Hebrews 4:15-16, Ephesians 6:18, James 4:2)

Prayer Resources:

http://www.thewordteaches.com/The_Word_Teaches/how_to_pray_biblic ally.htm http://www.bible.ca/ntx-prayer.htm http://mbogartministries.hubpages.com/hub/Praying-for-People-Biblically http://xacentral.com/resources/files/ActsPrayer.pdf

C.  *Understand what God is like.* Learn what God's attributes are and how that teaching applies to your life. How can you draw close to someone when you don't know what they are like? If you don't know what He is like then you won't know how reliable He is when you need His help. God reveals Himself in specific ways so we can understand Him and His ability to help us as well as understand us and be able to meet our needs.

1.  Because God is *personal Spirit,* we understand that life is designed to build relationship with Him. As humans we can't feel Him or see Him.

2.  Because God is *all powerful* He is my help in every situation. There is nothing too hard for Him.

3.  Because God is *omnipresent* He is always right there, and personally knows what is happening in my life. He knows my failures, my hardships, my concerns, my problems. He is there to walk with me through life, especially those tough times.

4.  Because **God knows everything**, He always knows what is happening in my life and He has a purpose for me. He knows how to make something out of a messed-up life, and how to get me through this difficulty I am facing. He knows my limits and what will best develop me, as well as what prepares me for the future. We may not understand why he is allowing something in my life, but he knows how that preparation will get me ready for some future ministry.

5.  Because God is *sovereign* He has freedom to do what he wants with me and is not responsible to let me know what is going on. This tells us that we must trust Him implicitly and submit to what happens in our life. The Sovereign God is in control. Our job is not to know what He is doing. Our job is to trust this Sovereign God and submit to Him.

6.  Because God is *holy* I must respond to my situation in a way that honors His being. God said because He is holy we must be holy. We must not only move away from sin and progress into a consistently righteous lifestyle. God's holiness means that He is and shall always remain faithful to his claims of who He is.

7.  Because God is *absolute truth* I must believe what He says even when my emotions doubt Him. The world entices us with lies to follow unrighteous ways and live in a compromised lifestyle. We are to be truth

22

seekers, for then we understand God. Jesus declared "I am the way, the truth..." John 14:6.

8. Because God is *righteous* I can believe He will always do right.
9. Because God is *just* He will properly deal with those who mistreat and harm us, and He will make right all injustice. We can fully forgive because we realize that God will make right the wrongs done against us.
10. Because God is *love*, He is unconditionally committed to my well-being. Because He is love, he calls us to love others, especially those who have wronged us. We are not only called to love our brothers and sisters in Christ, but also love our enemies. We can love because we are loved.
11. Because God is *faithful*, I can trust Him to always keep His promises.
12. Because God *never changes* I can always count on Him. That is His character. Perfection does not have to change.

Check out these websites that help you understand the attributes of God:
http://preceptaustin.org/attributes_of_god.htm
http://www.pbministries.org/books/pink/Attributes/attributes.htm
http://www.allaboutgod.com/attributes-of-god.htm

D. *Learn how to obey God.* This is what will give your life dynamics. The more you learn to live in God's will the more you will enjoy life, and the more you will get out of life. Obedience is an expression of your love for God. Obedience will give you the greatest benefits in life and will help you gain the most rewards in heaven. Obedience will help you understand God better. He gave us His word and when we live it out we tend to understand the mind of God better. Obedience actually helps us understand God's word. You obey in one area and something makes more sense in another. (Amos 3:3; John 14:15, 21, 15:14; I John 2:3-6; Luke 6:46; Ephesians 2:10, 4:1, 4:17, 5:2, 8, 15; Matthew 16:24-26)

E. *Learn how to share your faith.* All who are saved are called to point out God's ways to others. We are God's witnesses to the world. How to do this is addressed in another section. We are also called to be lights in this world. (Witnesses: Proverbs 11:30, James 5:19-20; Matthew 28:19-20, Acts 1:8, 22:15; 1 Peter 3:15 Light: Matthew 5:14-16; Ephesians 5:8; Colossians 1:12-13)

F. *Learn how to maintain your fellowship with God.* All believers come into fellowship with God at salvation. Value your fellowship and relationship with God and maintain it. (Revelation 3:20; John 17:3; 1 John 1:3, 5-7) Paul's overwhelming desire was to get to know God more and more through the experiences of life. (Phil 3:10; see also V. 12-15) Sin hinders fellowship with God. (Psalm 66:18, Isaiah 59:2; I John 1:5-9) After one is saved a Christian needs to confess their sins daily. Sin, no matter how bad it is, after salvation does not terminate your salvation; it hinders your fellowship with God until you confess it. Knowing how to properly deal with sin is a key to maintain fellowship with God. Satan loves to do what he can to hold people in bondage because of their failures. Carefully notice the details of the following verse.

*"If we confess our sins, He is faithful and just to forgive us our sins, and to cleanse us from all unrighteousness." I John 1:9*

1. We are told to confess our sins which mean we recognize sin for what it is and acknowledge it to God. We call our sin by name; lust, greed, rage, sexual impurity, fear, disobedience, cheating, name calling, etc.
2. God's response is based in his faithfulness and justice. He is faithful to forgive, and his forgiveness is always based on His just response. Full and complete payment was made for our sin by Jesus.
3. Notice that we are cleansed from ALL unrighteousness. There are important truths that you need to be aware of when you sin. David wrote his process of confessing his sin of adultery to God in Psalm 51 when he said *"Against you, and you only, have I sinned, and done that which is evil in your sight;"* Every sin we commit is against God. You offend God by your sin each time. When Nathan accuses King David of his sin of adultery, he acknowledges his sin immediately and David was told right away that he was forgiven. (2 Samuel 12:13) You are always immediately forgiven when you confess your sins.
4. Not only are you forgiven that sin you acknowledged, but any other offense that you didn't recognize or know about that offends God is also cleansed or forgiven.
5. Confession can go like this: *"God I responded in anger to my spouse, and that was wrong."* Be specific in naming your sin and then accept God's forgiveness. Don't wait to feel forgiven, accept it and then thank God for his forgiveness each time. Living by faith means that we believe what God tells us, and here He tells us that if we confess, He forgives us from all sin. When forgiven you are then in fellowship with God whether you feel like it or not. Don't doubt the authority of God's word. If God has forgiven your sin and you still have guilt then it is not God reminding you of your failure. There is one who is a liar who will taunt you with your unworthiness to be forgiven and your failure.

G. *Develop and maintain fellowship with believers.* There has been a unity established with other believers in your faith. You are now brothers and sisters in Christ. (John 1:12. Ephesians 4:1-6) It takes effort on your part to establish and maintain such fellowship. One of the places God has ordained to establish such relationships is the local church. Church is not just for your benefit, but also an opportunity for you to have positive influence in the lives of other believers. Make church a regular part of your weekly schedule. (Hebrews 10:24-25; John 15:18-19; Ephesians 4:11-12; 1 Corinthians 12:13-26)

H. *Use your Spiritual Gift.* God has given every believer a spiritual gift at the moment of their salvation. Spiritual gifts are abilities to use with our talents and passion to build up and encourage other believers. What can you do to reach the lost or help believers grow? Learn what the gifts are and which gift the Spirit has given you and then seek to develop your gift. Google "Spiritual gift assessments". Take 2-3 of them and see where your strengths are. Don't forget to read the furnished definitions on these sites that describe the gifts. Gifts are listed in the following places: I Corinthians 12:1-7, 11; 1 Corinthians 12:8-10, Romans 12:3-8, Ephesians 4:11-15 1 Peter 4:8-11. Here are two sites where you can take a spiritual gift inventory and see what your gift is. http://www.churchgrowth.org/cgi-cg/gifts.cgi?intro=1--    http://www.d-m-m.org/support-files/giftstest.pdf

When you recognize what your gift is, then recognize that as your calling to a specific area of service. Serving God and others is really an important way to grow. In fact it should be recognized that Christians who don't serve will not mature to the same level as those who serve God and others. Don't excuse yourself from serving God in some capacity through your church or in your place of work or school. Get started just as soon as you can. Experiences help form you in your faith.

I. *Choose a good church to attend.* What should you look for in a good church? It should be a place where the Word of God is taught faithfully. It should be a place where you can exercise your spiritual gift in service to others. It should have a strong emphasis on missions and worldwide evangelization. It should reach out into your community. Realize that the people won't be perfect there and will offend you on occasion, but learn how to put your faith into practice in each situation in life. It should be a church in which you enjoy the fellowship of the people. Check out: http://www.gotquestions.org/find-local-church.html

As you think about going to church to worship God, one of the things you will want to do is seek to understand the style of worship that best connects you with God. There is a test on worship styles. Check it out and discover your style. http://common.northpoint.org/sacredpathway.html

J. *Develop a circle of godly friends.* Develop friendships with people who have been in the faith for some time and are also mature Christians. Realize that their maturity doesn't make them perfect. They will fail you, but don't let that detour you from your purpose for God. Such friends will answer questions for you, and give you ideas of how to live out your faith and work through your problems. You can learn a lot by watching how people react to life and express their faith in the world. When you fail they will lift you up and encourage you to continue on with your walk with God. They will help make your ideals and faith practical.

Explore websites, sermons and YouTube messages that talk about friendships and mentoring. http://www.crosswalk.com/faith/spiritual-life/how-christian-women-can-mentor-and-be-mentored-1409871.html http://communicate.mx/godly-friends-and-friendship

K. *Walk in the Spirit.* The Holy Spirit lives in you and is there to help you in life. Learn how to be sensitive to the Spirit's leading. The Spirit-led life is what empowers us to be different, to be able to change, to become more like Christ, to understand God's word, and to do great things for the cause of God. (Galatians 5:16, 22-25; Ephesians 6:18; 1 Thessalonians 5:19)

Check out such sites as these:
http://powertochange.com/experience/spiritual-growth/walkinspirit1/
http://bible.org/seriespage/spirit-filled-life-part-2

# Chapter 5 - DEFENSE OF YOUR FAITH

It is not only important to know what you believe as presented in chapter one. You also need to know why you believe what you do. This is called "apologetics". It means you learn how to defend what you believe. You learn how to express the "whys" of your faith to others. How do you know there is a God? Why do you believe that Jesus is the only way to God? Why do you believe that Jesus is God? Why do you believe in the resurrection? Why do you believe the Bible is the Word of God? In Revelation 2-3 churches were commended by Christ for having stood for their faith when people opposed them or brought in false doctrine.

Many young people turn from their faith in college, because their faith is challenged, and they don't know how to defend their faith in a logical manner. Just because we are people of faith doesn't mean there isn't logic and evidence behind what we believe. We do not have a blind faith but a faith based in substance. We can't see God, but there is the substance of God's revelation in nature, in the Bible, in Jesus Christ, and in the way Christianity changes the lives of its followers for the better and gives them purpose beyond expectation. Philosophy asks the questions of life but often doesn't have the answers. Christianity has the answers to the tough questions of life.

*Atheists base many of their beliefs in blind faith*

Atheists want you to think they are great intellectuals, but in reality they are driven by blind faith. In their view of science they propose how the world began, but it is blind faith in how matter began. They can't explain the origin of matter.

Atheists have a blind faith when it comes to God. They have no evidence that God doesn't exist. They use only their reasoning with no solid evidence for their choice. They don't know how to examine the unseen and unknown world. Often they use their prejudiced arguments to defend their position.

Atheists have a blind faith when it comes to an afterlife. They can only use their reasoning, which has not based on evidence, to affirm or deny that there is a heaven or hell. They hope there is no hell. They hope that death ends all and we cease to exist at death. They hope there is no judgment. But intellectual reason does not change the realities of the unseen world.

Atheists have a blind faith that their actions will not be judged after death. By their own definition they can't use science on something they can't reproduce or examine. So, all their conclusions about any form of afterlife are based on a blind faith that has no resources upon which to draw such a conclusion. It's only their flawed intellectual reasoning. Therefore, they take strong stands based solely on their reasoned out opinion which, in reality is blind faith.

Learn to see the holes in their reasoning. Often their motivation for aggressive attacks against people of faith is to demean them or put us on the defense. If you are defending your faith then you can't challenge their thinking. Many will accuse you, belittle you, and even seek to humiliate you to avoid addressing the truth. Make sure you don't stoop to their level. Learn how to address the subject with logic, calm reason and faith. Don't back away from the teaching of God's word when they attack you. Learn to stand firmly with dignity. Don't ever resort to name calling.

With that said, please recognize that we also need to know how to defend what we believe. Below are simple defenses we can use for questions people have about the faith. Along the way I will give you web addresses and resources that offer deeper explanations about how to stand for your faith in specific areas.

A.  How do I know the Bible is the Word of God?

1.  It is crucial that you understand why you believe the Bible is the Word of God. If you understand this, it will give you confidence to stand for what the Bible teaches. The first truth we need to realize is that the Bible does claim to be God's word. (Hebrews 4:12; 1 Timothy 3:16, Matthew 5:18; 2 Peter 1:19-21; Psalm 119)

2.  All other religions had one person who wrote their holy book, and that was usually in one generation. God used over 39 different writers over a period of 1600 years, and yet it still presents a consistent picture of God and His plan for man through all its writers. Every other religion in the world requires people to perform good works to earn salvation. The Bible is the only holy book that does not require us to do good works in order to gain salvation. It presents a salvation that comes by the acceptance of Jesus as Savior and by personally acting on that truth through faith. (Acts 4:12) *"There is salvation, in none other, for neither is there any other name under heaven that is given among men, by which we must be saved!"* How do good works fit into the plan of God? Instead of gaining our

salvation by good works, we learn that God expects good works out of those who have already been saved by faith. (Ephesians 2:10)

The Bible is a book that shows a supernatural source. A quarter of the Bible is considered prophetic, telling us what will happen in the future. These prophecies were made shortly before things happened (walls of Jericho falling), some a generation before they happened, (division of Israel into two nations given to Solomon) as well as hundreds of years before they happened (the prophecies about Christ). Most prophecies have been fulfilled in his birth, life, death and resurrection, but many have not yet been fulfilled. The book of Revelation and much of Daniel, some of Ezekiel, and Zachariah 14, are yet to be fulfilled.

Concerning the first coming of Christ, His person, and His work, there are over 100 prophecies that were fulfilled by Him. Just try coming up with twelve prophecies about a person who will become famous 300 years from now. Tell where he will be born, what family line he will come through, what kind of things he will do, how he will die and how his life will affect the people of the world. Some of the prophecies of Christ start right after the fall of man, some came from Moses (1500 BC), some from David (950 BC), some from Isaiah (700 BC) and some from Zachariah (500 BC). They were literally fulfilled. No other holy book or prophet has the Bible's track record for accuracy.

Prophecies of Christ:
http://www.godandscience.org/apologetics/prophchr.html
http://www.godonthe.net/evidence/messiah.htm

*The science of archaeology* has found no discoveries that have disproved any aspect of the Bible. Not everything mentioned in the Bible is backed up by archaeological finds, but nothing has been discovered that disproves it either. I was told that 20 years ago by an archaeologist who spoke at a seminar I attended. I find it interesting that this very truth is mentioned in the opening paragraphs of the first website listed below.

Check out such places as:
http://www.biblelight.org/arch1.htm
http://christiananswers.net/archaeology/

Every other representative of each religion died and is still in the grave. Jesus died with a purpose, (to provide redemption for man) and then rose from the dead to prove that He made full payment for man's sin. Jesus is shown to be God by his claims (over 214 times in the Gospel of John alone), His unique teachings and by the miracles He did. Christianity is the only religion that shows us God and His true nature in human form and gives us God's view on life.

Every other religion is a list of do's and don'ts to appease a terrifying god or an unknown or even non-existent being. Christianity is a religion in which its established purpose is a relationship with God in which love, mercy, grace, kindness and help are the qualities people experience. He calls us his children and invites us to live in His home for all eternity in an intimate relationship with Him. Christianity offers a relationship with God. Jesus (who is God) declared that eternal life is knowing God intimately. (John 17:3) *"This is eternal life, that they should know you, the only true God, and him whom you sent, Jesus Christ."* The Bible is unique in the message of love. What religion do you know that has such an emphasis on love and relationships with God? It is indeed different from every other religion.

The teachings of the Bible have caused Christians to do more to change the world in a positive way than any other religion. Christianity has established and promoted education, scientific research, hospitals, orphanages and convalescence homes. Great works of art and great music have their sources from the Bible. Christian music is some of the most upbeat and positive music in the world. Every religion portrays man pursuing God for acceptance through their good works. The Bible presents God pursuing man and offers the gift of salvation in which there is reconciliation with the God they offended. It is, indeed, different and of higher quality and character than any other religion in the world.

3.  It's a book of consistently high moral character. Not all people portrayed in the Bible are of great moral character. Even the good ones are pictured as they are, and their lives are not white-washed to be something they aren't. Yet God continues to value them even though they fail.

4.  It is a book that speaks about the future with such authority indicating that the one behind it has a unique knowledge of the future. Such teachings include predictions about the birth, work, death and return of Christ. (Psalm 22; Isaiah 53; Zechariah 14)

5.  It addresses issues of the future with specific detail that only someone who knows what is behind the curtain of death can speak about it so plainly and with such certainty. The Bible speaks about such things as death, heaven, hell and judgment day that we have no other way of

knowing about these truths other than through a revelation from God. Isaiah 46:9-10 *"Remember the former things of old; for I am God, and there is none other; I am God, and there is none like Me, declaring the end from the beginning, and from ancient times the things that are not yet done, saying, 'My counsel shall stand, and I will do all My pleasure,"*

*Check out*

http://carm.org/cut-bible
http://bible.org/article/why-i-believe-bible
http://www.christiananswers.net/q-eden/edn-t003.html

B.      *How do I know there is a God?*

1. He has revealed Himself in nature. By observing this world we recognize there has to be a designer and creator. (Romans 1:19-20, John 1:3, Colossians 1:16)

2. Accurate prophecy indicates someone exists who is unique and who knows the future. (Isaiah 46:9-10)

3. Miracles indicate there is a source of power greater than what man possesses. (John 6:1-24)

4. The intuitive knowledge of the existence of God (or a supreme being) is inborn in every person around the world. Why is there such universal knowledge if there is no God?

5. There is enough evidence of the existence of God seen in complexity and variety of creation to affirm His existence. But we must still accept His existence by faith.

Check out: http://www.christiananswers.net/q-aig/aig-c038.html
Check out this video: http://www.youtube.com/watch?v=YgJmsK2s0uI

C. *Isn't the Bible full of errors?* Ask the person to identify specific errors. Most people only hear about some, but they have never explored these alleged errors. People often speak out of ignorance. Even scholars who claim the Bible has errors do not say that it is full of errors. Just because they claim there are errors doesn't make it true.

1. Recognize there are some difficulties that take some study to reconcile. An apparent contradiction can often be cleared up by a little study or reading the text and placing it into its context. See http://www.answersingenesis.org/articles/am/v2/n4/isnt-the-bible-full-of-

errors -- http://www.josh.org/resources/study-research/answers-to-skeptics-questions/isnt-the-bible-full-of-contradictions/

    2. Archaeological research has consistently proven the accuracy of the Bible.

    3. There are some scribal errors, but these are recognized. Never do these affect any of the teaching of the Bible. In some places numbers do not match. These errors are recognized and not denied. None of these affect the teachings of the Bible.

D.    *Aren't there many ways to Heaven?* (You have your way and I have mine. What makes your way the only way?) Keep these facts in mind:

    1. God created earth and man; therefore all men are responsible to this God. There are not many gods, only one. This one God speaks of only one way that he has provided for man to enter heaven.

    2. Jesus died to provide redemption for ALL mankind, not just for the Jews or Christians. There was no other provision made by God for people to be saved. (Romans 5:8; Hebrews 7:25, 9:22-28)

    3. God has declared there is only one way to enter heaven. (John 14:6) When Jesus declares that "*No Man*" comes to the father but by Him, He is very emphatic. See also Acts 4:12 and 1 John 5:11-13. "He that has the Son has life and he that has not the son has not life." That really narrows down the way people can seek to enter heaven by God's standard.

E.    *How can a loving God send people to an eternal hell?*

    1. God is not just love but He is also righteous and therefore requires righteousness from mankind. He is holy and cannot tolerate sin. He is just and must punish sin. Even though He is merciful, loving and gracious, He cannot move toward us until his righteousness, holiness and justice has been satisfied. His love and grace have moved Him to act on our behalf to deliver us from hell, but he then leaves the choice with us as to whether we want to accept payment for our sins or pay for our own sins in hell for eternity. So people actually choose to go to hell when they reject God.

    2. To deny an eternal hell is to deny the teachings of Jesus and the Bible. The Bible warns about hell. It doesn't matter if a person accepts the teaching of hell or not. The fact is that this teaching is in the Bible, and Jesus, who is God, spoke most about it. If a person doesn't make proper preparation to avoid hell, then he has chosen his eternal destiny.

3. On what basis does one have to deny hell? It is not a matter of a person's choice. Denial does not change reality. They can reason hell away by saying that they don't believe a loving God could allow such a thing. They could reason it away as myth, or a method of fear the church uses to control people on earth. They think that rational thinking and logic is enough to make it go away. Their problem is that they have no authority or concrete evidence upon which to base their assumption. The Bible is God's revelation. He knows what is coming and what is awaiting each person. We should take His warnings in the Bible seriously.

4. Do we have a right to dictate what God is like? He not only is love, but He is also a holy. He is a just and jealous God. Think about the Flood and all the people who died because they were wicked. There were people that God told the Israelites to wipe out because of their wickedness. God also brought the Assyrians and the Babylonians against Israel and Judah to bring judgment on them, because they turned their back on God to live like the pagans around them. The book of Revelation talks about God's wrath being poured out on the people of the earth, with millions being killed in judgment through painful sores, stinging locust, or extreme heat. He inflicts impenetrable darkness against those who have rejected Him.

If you honestly read the Bible you notice that God does not take sin lightly, and he openly judged those who refuse to turn from their sin. Hell is a reminder that God will not hesitate to judge all those who reject reconciliation with Him and the Savior He has provided to allow them to escape sins penalty. We cannot make God in our image, or according to our specifications. We need to recognize who He is and that He is willing and committed to reject these people for eternity in a place called hell or the lake of fire. He has warned us about hell. If we try to deny hell by making God something that He is not, then we have created a false god to accommodate our rejection of hell.

Check out: http://www.leaderu.com/orgs/probe/docs/hell.html
http://carm.org/hell -- http://www.gty.org/Blog/B110430

F. *Is it logical to believe in miracles?* The real issue in this question is: "Does God exist?" If He does, then there is no problem with miracles. Does the God who created the world have the ability to do what would be supernatural to us? The creator is lord over His creation. God also claims to be all-powerful and actively involved in the affairs of man. Ask why the skeptic doubts that God is capable of intervening in the affairs of man. http://christiananswers.net/q-aiia/aiia-miracles2.html  --

http://www.josh.org/resources/study-research/answers-to-skeptics-questions/how-can-miracles-be-possible/

G.     *Why does God allow the righteous to suffer?* It seems logical to think that because we belong to an all powerful God that we should be exempt from suffering if we are faithful to him. There are various reasons for suffering. It is a means of growth, chastening, training, purging, and God's glory. (See James Dobson's Book <u>When God Doesn't Make Sense</u> and <u>The Problem of Pain</u> by C.S. Lewis)

*Resources*: Websites that will answer your questions and how to go about defending your faith. Many of these sites will help you when you talk with skeptics about your faith.

a.   http://www.apologetics.com/
b.   http://carm.org/apologetics
c.   http://www.summit.org/resources/
d.   http://www.apologetics315.com/
e.   http://www.rzim.org/
f.   Authors who can start you off in this discipline of Apologetics: Josh McDowell's <u>Evidence That Demands a Verdict</u>, Charles Carlson's <u>How Now Shall We Live</u>, Lee Strobel's <u>The Case for Faith</u>, <u>The Case for Christ</u>, <u>The Case for the Resurrection,</u> <u>The Case for the Creator,</u> "<u>The Case for Easter</u>. If you are not a reader, then look for some of these books in audio format. The online Bible has some good free modules on creation and evolution as well as world view. Get the free Bible and then add the modules you like. This Bible program is helpful for apologetics. Find it at http://onlinebible.net/

# Chapter 6 - DETERMINING THE QUESTIONABLE AREAS OF LIFE

The Bible is specific in many areas as to what is right or wrong, but how does one make decisions about topics not specifically addressed in the Bible? In those cases the Bible gives us principles by which to make such decisions in determining if grey areas are right or wrong. Whom will you marry? What kind of job does God want you to pursue? Is it wrong to hang out in a bar? Biblical principles will not always lead people to the same decision in every situation. Romans 14 talks about some actions being wrong for immature Christians and acceptable for more mature Christians. Remember this is addressing those undefined areas, not areas in which the Bible is specific.

https://bible.org/seriespage/strong-and-weak-romans-14

There are many things that are not questionable, because they are well defined. Does God want you to marry that person who is not saved? 2 Corinthians 6:14 answers that. Is it acceptable to have sex outside of marriage? 1 Corinthians 6:13-20 and 1 Thessalonians 4:3-8 are very specific. We don't have to wonder about what God has forbidden us to do. However, there are areas of life that are not specifically addressed. These are the undefined areas of life and faith. That is the purpose of this section. Here are Biblical principles for determining what to do in those undefined areas of your Christian life:

A.      *Make sure your life is dedicated to the Lord* and you are committed to seeking His way. This allows you to make a decision based on honoring God by the outcome rather than based on your desire and the pressure of the moment. (Proverbs 3:5-6, Romans 12:1-2) How can you expect God to lead you if you only want to know His will so you can consider doing it or not? Be committed to following the Lord no matter what he wants you to do. If your life is dedicated to God you will want to honor God. (Mark 8:34-38)

B.      *Is what you want to do called sin?* If it is called sin, then you know God's will right away about what to do or not do. God's will never include any kind of sin as an acceptable direction for your life. (Romans 6:12-13) If sin is part of what you choose, then realize that mingling sin with righteousness does not impress God. If what you want to do is called sin, then realize that the offensive nature of sin will not help you draw closer to God in any way, nor will it be of benefit to you.

C. *Will it lead you into sin?* Some things you choose may not start off to be sin, but it could strongly influence you into sin. An example might be spending time with wrong people. They could lead you into sin. Do those people regularly pressure you to compromise your beliefs? (Romans 13:12-14; Psalm 1:1-2)

D. *Will it cause my brother in Christ to stumble and fall?* Something may be all right for me, but it may cause my brother in Christ to falter in his walk of faith. We should avoid such practices for the sake of our brother. It may not bother you to drink a beer, but it may influence a weaker brother to indulge and not be able to control himself. (Romans 12:13) Make yourself familiar with Romans 14 for it is a key passage in helping you to establish priorities when making such a consideration.

E. *Do I have faith to do it and believe it is not sin?* There are some things that may be all right for me to do, but I feel guilty doing them. I ought to elude such behavior. (Romans 14:23)

F. *Will what I do glorify God?* How would I feel if Jesus were watching me do this? (He always is!) Would I feel uncomfortable if Jesus were standing next to me when I do this? Many people over the years stop swearing when they found out I was a pastor. My presence made them feel differently about their speech. Do you honestly think about the fact that God is always with you listening to your every word and even knowing your thoughts and motives? Do I feel this will glorify God? Is this what I want to be doing when Jesus returns? Remember that our purposes should have an eternal perspective in which we want to honor God. (Romans 15:6; I Corinthians 1:31; Colossians 3:17, 23)

G. *Will what I am doing build up my brother in Christ?* My actions should do more then not lead him into sin; it should have a positive quality that gives an example of seeing a person devoted to pleasing God by his or her life. People learn from example as much as from words. Do they observe your attitude of wanting to honor God? When they see you doing right they can then seek to emulate what they see in you. Are you concerned that your actions will build others up in the Lord? (Romans 14:19; 15:2; Ephesians 4:29)

*Here are some things to think about when considering if something is right:*

A. Would Jesus do this? (*Philippians2*:1; Romans 8:29)

B. Does it disturb me to realize that God is watching me? (Proverbs 15:3)

C. Would this benefit me on judgment day? What is the eternal value of what I am doing? (2 Corinthians 5:10; I Corinthians 3:11-15)

D. Would I be embarrassed to have godly people I know see me do this?

E. Will I still be glad I did this or made this choice in 500 years?

F. Am I quenching the Spirit when I do this? (I Thessalonians 5:19)

G. Does this activity/choice leave me with a clear conscience when I want to pray? (Acts 24:16)

H. Does this activity/choice benefit or detract from the goal of Christian growth in my life? (2 Peter 3:18)

I. Have I honestly prayed about what God wants me to do? Have I taken the time to listen for God's response after I made my request? (Colossians 1:9)

J. If you decide to do something and do it, do you still have peace after participating in it for a period of time, or are you repressing guilt? You must be honest with yourself on this one. (Luke 1:79, Romans 12:18, 14:17, Philippians 4:9, 1 Corinthians 7:15, Ephesians 1:2)

K. Would this please God? (Colossians 1:10)

L. If God were visible in your presence, would you think differently about what you were doing?

JSO-8/92

# Chapter 7 – CREATOR IN OUR FAITH

Creation is not an obscure notion in the Bible but a major doctrine and teaching. Included here is only a small sampling of references to the Creator references in the Bible. Recognizing God as the creator of all things is a recognition of His Lordship over not just the earth but all humanity. It is recognizes His right to established a unified moral standard over all humanity. This means that all are responsible to come to God on His terms, not on their own terms. This is a very important subject. To not recognize God as the creator means that man becomes his own source of authority in how he runs his life. (Emphasis in verses added by author)

1. (Genesis 1:1) In the beginning *God created* the heaven and the earth.

2. (John 1:3) *All things were made by him*; and without him was not anything made that was made.

3. (Genesis 2:4) These are the generations of the heavens and of the earth *when they were created*, in the day that *the LORD God made the earth and the heavens.*

4. (Genesis 5:1) This is the book of the generations of Adam. In the day that *God created man, in the likeness of God made He him.*

5. (Deuteronomy 4:32) "For ask now of the days that are past, which were before thee, since the day that God created man upon the earth, and ask from the one side of heaven unto the other whether there hath been any such thing as this great thing is, or hath been heard like it?

6. (Isaiah 42:5) Thus says God Yahweh, he who created the heavens and stretched them out, he who spread out the earth and that which comes out of it, he who gives breath to its people and spirit to those who walk in it.

7. (Isaiah 45:18) For thus says Yahweh who created the heavens, the God who formed the earth and made it, who established it and didn't create it a waste, who formed it to be inhabited: "I am Yahweh; and there is no other.

8. (Malachi 2:10) Have we not all one father? *Has not one God created us?* Why do we deal treacherously every man against his brother, by profaning the covenant of our fathers?

9. (Mark 13:19) For in those days shall be affliction, such as was not from the beginning of the creation which God created unto this time, neither shall be.

10. (Colossians 1:16) For by him were *all things created*, that are in heaven, and that are in earth, visible and invisible, whether they be thrones, or

dominions, or principalities, or powers: *all things were created by him, and for him.*

11. (Revelation 4:11) You are worthy, O Lord, to receive glory and honor and power: *for you have created all things, and for thy pleasure they are and were created.*

12. Other Passages: Job 4:17; 20:4; 26:7, 13; 33:4; 36:3; Ecclesiastes 11:5; 12:1; Isaiah 37:16; 40:28; 41:20; 42:5; 43:1; Jeremiah 10:12; 14:22; 31:35; 32:17; 33:2; Ezekiel 29:2; Romans 1:19-20, 25

Implications of recognizing God as creator

A. God claims to be the exclusive creator as declared in the Bible. If He is not, then He is a liar. If Bible writers made a mistake on this issue, then how do we know anything else they said is true?

B. Creation is God's basis of authority over man. If He created us then He can place responsibility and restriction upon us. If man evolved, he is his own boss.

C. Creation in the Bible is best expressed by the word "ex-nihilo" which means to bring into being from nothing. That cannot be manipulated to mean evolution in any way. To acknowledge God as Creator is to recognize that He knows our every need and how we best function.

D. To acknowledge God as Creator is to recognize that He knows our every need and how we best function. The designer knows what will bring the greatest benefit to us.

E. To recognize God as our creator is to recognize that we are responsible for our actions to this One who is our maker. Because he has given us free will we can make our own choices, but there are also consequences which we choose by those actions.

F. To accept Creation as presented in the Bible is to accept the witness of the one who was there when it happened.

JSO - 8/92

*If creation is true what would you expect to see in research?*
A. Sudden appearance of fully developed animals and man.
B. Intelligent man from the beginning.
C. Changes within a kind but still maintaining basic similarities, e.g. the dog (4 feet, bark, etc.)
D. Complex design in the creatures.
E. Variety that shows the creator was intelligent and imaginative.

F. A revealed record would not be out of line. He would want man to know his origin. This Creator who gave us intelligence to learn would also have the ability to communicate with us.

G. Innate sense of belonging.

H. Design and interdependence of creation.

I. Purpose for mankind seen in vegetation, minerals and resources in the world. Each plant has specific and meaningful purposes for mankind, animals, insects and fish?

*If evolution is true what would you expect to see in research?*

A. Animals, plants and man still in transition and new species coming into existence.

B. Abundant intermediary fossils leading to new species. Scientists tell you that evolution is slow, and so there ought to be time for a fossil record to show this change. Why is it lacking?

C. Deformity. Changes and body parts come by random selection or deformity rather than purpose.

D. The appearance of a realistic mechanism that causes the change that brings about macro-evolution, that is, change in species.

E. Indisputable evidence of an old earth, sun and moon.

F. Things getting better rather than running down

G. Second law of thermo dynamics found not to be true.

H. Inner breeding bringing about new classifications of animals.

I. Major changes still taking place and clearly evident in plants and animals.

Check out some of the creation websites: http://www.answersingenesis.org/
Institute of Creation Research: http://www.icr.org/ http://creation.com/
Good resource book: **Darwin on Trial** by Philip E. Johnson.

# Chapter 8 - SINS AGAINST YOUR FAITH

The Bible says that we are all sinners. We all struggle with sin and becoming a believer does not exempt us from this struggle with sin. Sin is ingrained in our nature, and we are totally depraved. That means that every part of our being is affected by sin. The Christian has been given the power to overcome sin, and to live separate from sin. A Christian who refuses to deal with personal sin will experience the discipline of God. (Read Hebrews 12) In Romans 6-8 it speaks of the kind of struggle we all face with sin. To live under the power of sin is to become a slave to it.

Christians have the ability in their faith to overcome sinful temptation and walk in righteousness. God has empowered us to overcome sin through the indwelling Holy Spirit, as well as the application of the teachings of God's word. God doesn't want us to cover our sins to make ourselves look good. He wants us to own up to our sins, confess them, overcome them and do what is right. Keeping a sin private gives it greater power over you. Find a mature Christian you can talk with about your struggles.

There are several words that describe various aspects of our failure to God. (Definitions are taken from the Online Bible, Strong's Hebrew and Greek modules.)

1. *Sin* (hamartono - Strongs # 264) to miss the mark. Morally, to miss God's mark of perfection or what is right. *Failing to do what God requires of us.*

2. *Iniquity* (Anomia # 459) A violation of the law, wickedness, transgression of the law, unrighteousness. *Perverting what is good.*

3. *Trespass* (Pesha # 06588) Transgression against individuals or God. Go over the boundary. *Insisting on doing what is forbidden*

4. *Guile* (Remeeyaw # 07423) Deceit, slothful, false, guile, a trick (bait) subtlety. *Projecting what is false.*

5. *Evil* (Rarah # 07451) Evil, to degenerate from original virtue, grievous, lewd, malicious, wicked bad, hurtful. Wickedness, mischief, hurt, trouble, affliction. *Actions not being what they should be.*

Righteousness is conforming to God's standard.

Because of the evolutionary philosophy being so strong today people are saying that we can't tell others what is right or wrong. They deny any kind of universal standard of morality. The Bible claims a moral standard by which all will be judged. We need to know what offends God so we can avoid it, and then stand for what is right, and do it.

There are many things the Bible calls sin. It is not our prerogative to determine what is right or wrong. God has clearly revealed in the Bible specific sins that offend His character. This list is not exhaustive but is here to help you know what the Bible says about specific sins. God does not tell us why these are wrong, but if we are observant in life, we can see how such sins harm not only our own life, but the lives of others, as well as society.

ADULTERY
  Exodus 20:14
  Leviticus 20:10
  Matthew 5:27-28
  1 Corinthians 6:12-17
  Galatians 5:19
  1 Thessalonians 4:3-8
  Hebrews 13:4

ABORTION
  Genesis 9:6
  Exodus 20:13
  Deut 27:25
  Psalm 139:13-16
  Proverbs 6:16-17
  Isaiah 49:1-3
  Jeremiah 1:4-5
  Luke 1:15, 44
  Luke 1:31-32

DRUNKENESS
  Proverbs 20:1
  Proverbs 21:17
  Proverbs 23:31
  Proverbs 31:4
  Isaiah 5:11
  Romans 13:13; 14:21
  Galatians 5:21
  Ephesians 5:18
  1 Timothy 3:3
  Titus 1:7

FILTHY TALK
  Exodus 20:7
  Matthew 12:34-37; 15:11-20
  Ephesians 4:29; 5:4
  Colossians 3:8
  James 3:10

GREED
  Ephesians 5:5
  1 Timothy 6:10
  Hebrews 13:5

HOMOSEXUALITY
  Genesis 13:13
  Genesis 19:4-10
  Leviticus 18:22
  Judges 19:22-23
  1 Kings 14:24; 15:11-12
  Romans 1:26-27
  1 Corinthians 6:9-11
  2 Peter 2:6
  Jude 1:7-8

LYING
  Proverbs 6:16-17
  Proverbs 13:5
  John 8:44
  Ephesians 4:25
  1 Timothy 1:10
  Revelation 21:8

PORNOGRAPHY
   (Same as adultery) *Matthew 5:27-
   28
   Proverbs 23:7
   Philippians 4:8
   1 Thessalonians 4:5
   1 John 2:16
   Revelation 9:20-21

LISTS OF SINS
   Proverbs 6:16-19
   Matthew 15:18-20
   Mark 7:20-23
   Romans 1:28-32
   1 Corinthians 6:9-11
   Galatians 5:19-21

Ephesians 4:25-32; 5:3-5
Colossians 3:5-9
2 Timothy 3:1-5
Revelation 21:8

MORAL CODE FOR YOUR FAITH
   Exodus 20:1-17
   Matthew 5:20-48
   John 15-16
   Romans 12-14
   Galatians 5:22-23
   Ephesians 4:24-32
   Colossians 3:10-23
   1 Thessalonians 4:3-8
   2 Peter 1:4-8

Some verses give us non-specific sins by identifying wrong values in our life.

1. Romans 14:23 "But he who doubts is condemned if he eats, because it isn't of faith; and whatever is not of faith is sin."

2. James 4:17 "To him therefore who knows to do good, and doesn't do it, to him it is sin."

3. James 5:17 "All unrighteousness is sin, and there is a sin not leading to death."

4. 1 John 3:15 "Whoever hates his brother is a murderer, and you know that no murderer has eternal life remaining in him."

JSO-7/92

45

# Chapter 9 - Worldview and how it affects you

Your worldview determines your values. It sorts out what is important from what is not. Understanding your worldview helps you know what stands to take in life, and it helps you understand why someone takes the positions they do. The more you understand the reason why people take specific stands, the easier it is to effectively address the underlying issues of their beliefs.

We started off this book with doctrinal truths taught in the Bible. These statements actually constitute the basis of the Christian worldview. Doctrine must be understood so it can affect your life and beliefs.

*"Everything we do in life is based on a set of presuppositions about the nature of reality, how things work, the meaning of life, what is important, and what is possible. Taken together, our presuppositions are called our worldview. This is the foundation, or framework, for interpreting life, for making decisions. It is a roadmap, a guide for getting around in life, for interpreting reality, and for making choices that have substance."*

*"A worldview is a way of looking at life. It is the framework into which we fit our beliefs and ideas, our ways of doing things, and judgments concerning truth and error, right and wrong. A world view attaches meaning and purpose to history, and assigns values to persons, objects, and events."* (Taken from: A Sure Foundation 2000 SMI Health Care Bible Study. http://www.thesmi.org/HCBS/hcbs2.PDF Used with permission)

*Here's a worldview personal study project:* Determine a worldview for yourself by using the Bible as your standard. Read through the first 12 chapters of Genesis. Then reread it noticing and recording the truths that should determine how you are to view the world. As you record your observations from these chapters, you will come to understand the worldview God has established that he wants you to know in order to regulate life. For some it is easier to do this project by having an example to follow. Let me share with you some of my findings as I worked on this project myself some years ago:

1. 1:26 God created man. We were designed and created in the image and likeness of God. We were made to rule over the earth. If we are a product of chance, then we are nothing but a higher form of animal. This statement helps us to see the worth of every person. We are made in God's image. Our value is not just in what we become, but also in who we are to God.
2. 1:27 God created the differences between man and woman. He made male and female differently and gave them the ability to see life in their unique

way. It was God that programmed them to be motivated by different perspectives in life and to have different functions.

3. 1:26-27, 3:8-9, 5:24, 6:6. By these statements we see that God is a personal, rational being, not an impersonal force. He is involved in the affairs of man.

4. 1:28 Having children is a part of God's plan. "*Be fruitful and multiply.*"

5. 1:29 Seed, plants and fruit are for food. If God designed them for us then they will meet specific purposes for nutrition, health and, even medication.

6. 2:3 God blessed the 7th day and made it holy, a day of rest and worship. God knows our need of physical rest and does not want us to always be taken up with work

7. 2:16-17. God established limitations for man. Some things are good, but some things are wrong. Such disobedience brings consequences. Disobedience in a specific area would bring death. God has the right to put restrictions on man. He did this from the very beginning. The purpose was so man could choose to be obedient and follow God.

8. 2:18 God recognized the need of a man to have a companion. Marriage and companionship is God's idea. God created woman to meet that need.

9. 2:22 God created woman to be a compliment to man and brought her to him. Woman was made for man to be his helper in life.

10. 2:24 God established marriage. This new tie would supersede one's ties with his parents and the couple would be joined together in this union. Sex was designed by God to be a part of the marriage relationship.

11. God, not man, is the one who established marriage. God designed sex to be part of the marriage relationship for procreation and pleasure.

12. God joined together a man and woman. Heterosexual relationship in marriage was God's design from the beginning.

13. You could also record the worldview from Gen 1-12 in short statements as in the following:

    a. There is a God and He is creator of all things.
    b. We are responsible to God.
    c. God is a personal God not an impersonal force.
    d. Both man and woman are important because they are made in God's image.
    e. Marriage is for a man and a woman.
    f. Marriage was instigated by God.
    g. God wants us to have children.
    h. Sin came into the world by disobedience.
    i. Death and suffering came as a result of sin.
    j. We are stewards of this earth and all on it.
    k. Our sin breaks our fellowship with God.

l.   We need redemption to be restored to God.

m.   God has provided only one way of redemption.

n.   Sin brings problems and makes people worse.

o.   God established human government.

A worldview is the framework from which we view reality and make sense of life and the world. *"[It's] any ideology, philosophy, theology, movement or religion that provides an overarching approach to understanding God, the world and man's relations to God and the world,"* says David Noebel, author of <u>Understanding the Times.</u> (Taken from: http://www.focusonthefamily.com/faith/christian_worldview/whats_a_christian_worldview.aspx)

Addressing the five topics below identifies one's worldview. Worldview is defined as any ideology, philosophy, theology, movement, or religion that provides an overarching approach to understanding God, the world, and man's relation to God and the world.

When determining what a person's worldview is, you can question them in the following areas:

1. Knowledge

   What is truth? What is the source of truth? Can we know anything with certainty? How do we know the things we know? Is truth the same for me as it is for you?

2. God

   Does God exist? Is it possible to know anything about Him? What is He like? Is God good? Is there more than one? Am I God? How does God relate to evil? How do I relate to God? Will God judge all mankind? Has he provided us with a basis for knowing him?

3. The Universe

   What is real? Why does "something" exist instead of "nothing?" Is the universe eternal or created? Does it have a purpose? Where did everything come from? Is the "natural" world all that exists, or is there a world beyond the natural world?

4. Man

   What makes a human a human? What happens after we die? Do we have a soul? Were we created for a purpose? What is the purpose of human history? Is human nature good, bad, or neutral? How are humans to relate to each other? Are we different from animals?

5. Ethics

   Is there such a thing as right and wrong? Who decides what is right and what is wrong? How do we know what is moral? Does absolute moral truth exist, or is it all relative? Is morality just opinion?

Taken from http://peaceyouthgroup.com/articles/worldview.htm (Used with permission)

Major world religions are based upon worldviews.

Hinduism is a worldview based upon many deities, an endless life-death cycle and inevitability of human suffering. Islam, on the other hand, is a religion of martyrdom, conquests by force, and police state modesty. Thus to understand any of these movements and religions, we must understand the worldview they are founded upon.

Islamic Worldview: http://www.allaboutworldview.org/islamic-worldview.htm

A secular worldview does not value human life. If all a child has ever been taught is that we are all accidents, is it really so unusual that there are so many abortions, murders and suicides in society? You can read more about it at: http://www.allaboutworldview.org/secular-worldview.htm

Worldview Chart

Resources: Summit Ministries offers an excellent Worldview chart that compares the beliefs of various worldviews held by various groups. They include: Biblical Christianity, Islam, Secular Humanism, Marxism-Leninism, Cosmic Humanism, and Postmodernism. Check it out.

http://www.summit.org/resource/worldview_chart/

Worldview Dictionary

Definitions are so important when understanding another person's point of view. How can we stand for what is right if we don't know the issues? How can we oppose wrong when we don't know how it is presenting itself in this world? Do you know what the implications are when accepting the "Politically Correct" philosophy of this world? Do you understand what people are saying when they tell you to be tolerant? Listen to Josh McDowell at James Dobson's Family Talk to learn about the real issues of this topic:

http://www.drjamesdobson.org/Broadcasts/Broadcast?i=1dfad606-8ec4-4c60-b9ab-4bfcf57a4905

Located at the following website is a dictionary that helps you to know terms that are used to describe various aspects of beliefs that present a portion of a worldview that opposes a Christian worldview. Bookmark this page.

http://www.summit.org/resources/dictionary/

## *Why is doctrine so Important to a correct worldview?*

A.    The doctrinal statement found in the first chapter is common to Christian organizations and churches. Why do Churches have doctrinal statements? What is the need? Few people read them or make them an important part of their life. Doctrine is the filter by which we interpret Scripture and view life and man's purpose on earth. It is a specific and legitimate worldview.

B.    What really is a doctrinal statement? It is a declaration of our worldview. It is a set of beliefs by which we understand life and what this world is about. Whether we realize it or not we use the teachings of the Bible to help us understand *what life is about*, what is *right or wrong*, and what is really important in life. If it is our worldview, it must then be the basis of the decisions we make. That is what the pastor seeks to do each week through his sermons.

C.    How does our doctrinal statement (chapter 1) create our worldview?

    1.    *The Bible is the Word of God:* The Bible declares our standard where right and wrong is defined. It reveals God to us, what life is about, where we came from and where we are going. It tells us what is right or wrong outside of our emotions. When we start redefining and reinterpreting our authority, such as the Bible, we set the groundwork for changing our worldview. We must have an authority to reveal what God's will is for all mankind. The Bible is our source of truth and is not determined by individuals, but revealed by God. It is authoritative for all humanity.

    2.    *The Godhead is One God Existing in Three Persons:* The Bible tells us there is a God, even though we can't see Him. We also learn that this God is the creator before whom all must one day give an account. Realizing God is our creator allows everyone to understand to whom we are responsible, and also that He has the right to tell us what to do. We learn that this God is different than anything we can fully grasp. Godhead is one God existing in three persons, unlike anything we can comprehend. God has always existed in relationship and salvation is God's offer for us to join in relationship with Him. The Bible reveals God in a specific way and we can't make up our own view of God. God has revealed Himself in only one way and we must seek to understand Him through his revelation. We need to make sure we have the right view of Him. Every religion that does not recognize God, as He has revealed Himself in the Scriptures, follows the wrong teaching.

3.    *The Person and Work of Christ:* The Bible teaches that God the Son came to earth as a man, lived a sinless life, revealed God to us so we can know what God is really like, and He has provided the only redemption possible for mankind. We learn that God the Son is on our side making intercession for us and preparing a place in heaven for us when we die. Jesus is the judge before whom all mankind will give account of their life. We don't make up the rules of what God will judge in us; we accept what He has clearly declared in the Bible.

4.    *The Person and Work of the Holy Spirit:* We learn that the Holy Spirit is also God and lives in Christians to help us understand the Bible, empowers us to live the Christian life, and to face life with God's power to help us live in a way that pleases God.

5.    *The Total Depravity of Man:* This teaching helps us to realize that because of our sin we are all separated from God, and we are totally incapable of doing enough good to make ourselves acceptable by God. Because of our sin we are doomed to an eternity of separation from God in a place called hell. When this is ignored men seek to make a salvation based on their own good works rather than the finished work of Christ. Because man seeks to cover the guilt of sin, he devises many religions and ways to God. Because we are sinners we have a strong attraction to sin. The sinfulness of man explains why there is so much evil in the world. Total depravity means every part of our nature is corrupt. We must put into our life a good system of checks and balances to keep sin under control. Atheistic teaching does not have a viable way of explaining the evil in the world.

6.    *The Teaching of Salvation:* This teaching focuses on how we relate to God's message of salvation. Man either seeks to earn God's favor or accepts it as a gift. Many people will seek to do good works in life to earn God's favor, and they are not doing it because they want to honor Him but win His favor. Salvation is based on the finished work of Christ on the cross. False teaching emphasizes people's quest for God through their own works and efforts. Their worldview makes up their own God or exalts their good works that keeps them out of heaven, and they remain the enemies of God. Other worldviews minimize the need of salvation or corrupt the very teaching of salvation.

7.    *Eternal Security of the Believer:* Our worldview of security in salvation affects the way we face our sins and failures. Knowing

we are totally accepted in God's presence gives us a peace in life and a confidence in our relationship with God and that nothing can separate us from Him.

8.  *Two Natures of the Believer:* Understanding this truth helps us to realize why we have a hard time living consistently as a Christian. Just because we are saved doesn't mean that we will always do everything right. Being saved doesn't mean that we don't have the capacity to do wrong and really bad things. When Christians don't understand that we have two natures, we then fail to understand why we are struggling so much to do what is right. Some think that when we are saved there should be no more struggles to do right. What they fail to realize is that the struggle is greater because now there is a greater battle to get us to live in a way that dishonors God. We will have this struggle until we die and are released from sin in heaven.

9.  *Church:* The teaching of the Church affects our worldview for it helps us to understand who we are. We are the bride of Christ, called to be holy and honor our groom, Jesus Christ. We are here with a mission and a purpose. We have been called to take the gospel to the world, and the church is God's method of reaching the world and building up the saints and caring for the needy. We are not to live in a way that brings dishonor to the groom. We are not to play the whore with the world and indulge in sinful gratification.

10. *Satan:* By understanding him, his ways and motivation, we realize why we have so many problems in this world, and why temptation to sin is so strong. We understand that we do have a spiritual enemy who is out to destroy God's people, get us off track, encourage us to embarrass the cause of God and not be concerned with those things that are eternal. Wars seem unending because Satan does all he can to take peace from people and to place people in bondage. There is a real devil that is the destroyer, deceiver, liar and murderer who totally hates God's children.

11. *Rapture and Second Advent:* The rapture is the coming of Christ *for* His saints to take us to heaven. The Second Coming is Christ coming *with* His saints to take over and rule the earth. This reminds us that there is coming a day when this world system will be destroyed and only Jesus will rule this earth. Christ gives us the privilege to be involved in ruling the earth. This world will not end by running out of energy, or having a great ice age, or by a

comet smashing into the earth and destroying civilization. God has a specific plan of how this age and this world are going to end. It will end in God's time according to his declared plan, not by accident.

12. *Eternal State:* This makes us realize that there is more to life than what is on earth. There is more at stake than how we get along in this life. How well will we prepare for the next life? There are consequences to disobeying God and not accepting His salvation. When we realize that at death we are all judged, and some go to hell while others go to heaven. That should affect the way we live. When we realize that God takes all His children to heaven, this gives hope in time of uncertainty and loss. Those who have no desire to please God have a free will to reject Him, and God will honor their choice. There are, however, certain horrible consequences to pay for their rejection of God and His way.

Articles about Worldview:
http://www.leaderu.com/orgs/probe/docs/w-views.html
http://bible.org/seriespage/essential-christian-worldview-what-truth-why-are-we-alive
http://www.biblicalworldview.com/a_instructor.html
http://carm.org/what-are-some-elements-christian-world-view
http://www.christianity.co.nz/truth2.htm
http://worldview3.50webs.com/index.html

Worldview tests to see where you are in your thinking and values:
http://www.worldviewweekend.com/test/register.php
http://www.worldviewweekend.com/test/test.php
http://www.quizfarm.com/quizzes/new/eddxii/what-is-your-world-view/
http://www.israelwayne.com/article3.htm

# Chapter 10 – A Self-examined Life

It is not unusual for employees of many companies to get annual performance reviews. Their work and accomplishments are evaluated, weaknesses are noted, improvement is planned and new direction is considered. Why do they do this? So their employees don't get stuck in a rut. Growth comes through honest evaluation, thoughtful planning and intentional actions to implement that plan.

Such evaluation is important for the Christian as well. Something that will help you stay on course in moving forward in your faith is to examine your life. Read the communion passage, *1 Corinthians 11:23-32,* and notice the specific requirement that God wants us to observe before we partake in communion (11:28). As you contemplate the death of our Lord, you are to examine your life. You are to judge your sin (11:29-32) and make sure you are progressing in your faith. God saved you for a purpose, and you need to be asking if you are walking in compliance to God's given purpose. Because deviations from our course are so subtle you need to check your progress and direction on a regular basis.

This section is very important, for it is foundational to maintaining a relationship with God. When we deal with specific sins, we are removing hindrances that prevent us from drawing close to this God, who is light and in whom there is no darkness at all. 1 John 1:5-7 speaks of the importance of walking in the light in order to have fellowship with God. Sin always hinders us from experiencing the best in life; it always causes us to miss the mark God has for us of living a productive, holy life. (Holy means to be separated from sin and devoted to God and His ways.)

This section concerning self examination is very important. Such self examination can make the difference between remaining a child or immature and progressing to a mature spiritually. As you raise children you tend to have to tell them everything they need to do. You discipline them because they are doing things they know they should not do. Children think that if they don't get caught almost anything is all right. Children have to be told to get up, get dressed, eat their meal, clean up after themselves, clean their room, do their chores, quit fighting with their siblings, and the list goes on.

As we mature we take responsibility for our own life. We clean up after ourselves, we set the alarm and get up on time, we hold down a job, and we take care of the children who don't know how to take care of themselves. We see things that need to be done, and we do them without being told. We see problems, and we fix them. We maintain relationships. Such things characterize a mature adult who is taking care of themselves and leading a productive life.

Being a mature Christian means that you assume responsibility for your life. The communion passage says that if we would judge our own lives we would not be judged by God (11:29-32). I had a man tell me one time that if I didn't convince him in my sermons of something that needed to be changed, he didn't feel he had to do it. That is the mark of immaturity He wasn't looking to bring about change in his life, he had to have someone tell him and convince him that those specific things were wrong in order for him to change.

One of the problems in legalistic churches is their people are told everything they have to do as well as the things you can't do. They take away the thinking process for their people. They do the work of the Holy Spirit, rather than allowing the Holy Spirit to do His work of convicting them of sin, guiding them in making correct choices, and choosing the proper course for their life.

When you take the time to question and examine your life, you are opening yourself up to the work of the Holy Spirit to convict you of sin and lead you in the path of righteousness. Such questioning sometimes humbles you and makes you realize how much you are off course.

1.  As we learn to make the course corrections for our life by ourselves, then we are proceeding as a mature Christian.

2.  When we intentionally apply what we learn from our Bible reading, or some specific truth we heard in Sunday's sermon, we are acting in a mature way.

3.  If we don't examine our life we will think everything is all right. We don't make course corrections to our life when we don't notice the sin or our wrong direction.

Every year I have a complete physical examination. It is in these examinations that the doctor can discover problems or potential problems. He then tells me of the course correction I need to make for my life. That is what church is about every week. Under the teaching of God's word we will see problems, or potential problems in our life, and we can then choose to make the needed course correction. When we do this regularly and before things get out of hand then it isn't a major issue to address. We need to be committed to doing self-examinations regularly so we can make those needed course corrections.

There is another issue I want to address about this matter of self examination. Sometimes we can get too critical of ourselves and think we are failing in every area. Be honest in your self-examination as you do this, and ask the Holy Spirit to make evident the specific area you need to focus your attention on that day or that week.

When you go through the following sections and find that you lack in specific areas, choose to focus on only one area of change in your life at this time. When we focus on too many areas of change we tend to get overwhelmed and we end up doing nothing. Focus on the one area that is the worst at this time. Often when we take care of the one with which we most struggle, it corrects other sins in our life. Take for instance that you decide to deal with your guilt caused by several wrongs you have done, and you want to make them right by asking forgiveness of people and/or make proper restitution. List the offenses and deal with the worst one first. Sometimes it is only a few you need to address. You are not going to be able to address every failure in your life. If the Holy Spirit gives you peace about the issues, turn your attention to moving forward in your life.

With all of that said, I now want to introduce a couple of methods of doing self-examination. The first method is presented in the first three sections. In section one you are given specific questions from the passage of scripture to use in self evaluation. This is to show you the process you can use in the next two sections.

Section two through three leave the process of developing questions with you. Use the scripture to formulate questions by which you examine your life. Your ultimate goal is to learn to use the scripture you are reading or studying to evaluate your life and formulate honest and tough questions that help you see the course corrections you need to make. If you do a lot of little course corrections, then you will find you don't need to make major course corrections later. Many people read the Bible like a novel. They read it and say, "That was good." And promptly walk away and forget what they have read. If you learn to read and formulate questions as you go along, then Scripture will stay with you and will accomplish what it was intended to do.

Section Four presents questions I formulated to help you do an evaluation of your life in areas you may not think about. Once you get used to doing such examinations, they will become more natural, and you won't need the list of questions here, because you will develop that habit of applying scripture to your life while you do your personal reading, studying or listening to messages. Choose the sections that apply to your immediate needs to start this exercise. Do section four first.

Learn to read through a passage and make it personal by writing questions that help you examine and evaluate your own life. Be honest with yourself when answering.

Section one: Romans 12 Examination of your life.
*Read the chapter and notice the question tied to the specific verse. Take as many days as you need to do this in a meaningful manner.*
-   Have I offered my body as a living sacrifice to God?
-   How am I learning to transform my mind from worldly thinking?
-   How do the next six verses help me define transformed thinking?
-   Do I think of myself more highly than I ought?

- Am I participating in the body to make it more effective?
- Am I using my gift to serve God? (*If you don't know what your gift is, then it is hard to know if you are doing so. See chapter 4, section H*)
- Do I love others as I should?
- Do I love evil or hate it? (*If I am continuing to practice evil, then that is an indication of my love for it.*)
- Do I show brotherly love to all the believers in my life?
- Do I trust God during my trials, or am I impatient and unwilling to trust God and live by faith?
- Do I rejoice in the hope I have in Christ, or am I depressed about how life is going?
- Am I faithful in prayer or is that a neglected area?
- Do I bless those who persecute me? Or do I blast them? How do my thoughts about them honor/dishonor God?
- Am I selfish or sensitive to others when I see them in need?
- Am I living in harmony with those that are in a different social class, or do I act superior to them and stand aloof to them and their needs? Am I judging them?
- How is sinful pride controlling me? Is pride keeping me from admitting my mistake? Does it prevent me from fully obeying God? Does it cause me to be controlling over people and/or value things more than people?
- Am I willing to associate with people of low position? Who are the people I refuse to fellowship with or with whom I don't want to have anything to do? Why is that? What makes me think I am better than others?
- Am I repaying people evil for evil? Do I seek to get even, hold a grudge or allow their evil to cause me to return evil to them? How do I need to change? Why do I justify such sin?
- Do I do right in the presence of all people? Am I living like a Christian before all people?
- Am I taking revenge? Or do I allow God to take vengeance? Do I trust Him to make things right? Do I really believe that He is committed to making things right?
- Am I overcoming evil with good?

Section Two: Are you maturing as a Christian? An Ephesians 4 study
  *Indicator One*: Mature Christians are characterized by their pursuit of unity. (Ephesians 4:2-6)
  *Indicator Two:* Mature believers are characterized by a desire to serve. (4:7-13)
  *Indicator Three*: Mature Christians are characterized by doctrinal stability. (4:14)

*Indicator Four:* Mature believers speak truthfully in the atmosphere of Christian love. (4:15)

Now use the verses in each of these sections to write your own questions for self-examination.

Section Three: Other Passages to develop on your own

The first section gave you the questions for the verses. The second section gave you a rough outline for you to do the work to formulate the questions. The third section just gives you the passage for you to do all the work on your own.

Following are other passages to go through and make personal by asking if you are living up to Biblical expectations in your life. If you go through each of these passages by doing a personal application and evaluation of your life, then it will help you develop a habit that will stay with you the rest of your life.

Make it a habit to take a chapter and pray your way through it. Set aside twenty minutes to an hour and go off by yourself to personalize the teachings of the chapter. Ask yourself if you are doing what it says. Read through the chapter or a portion of it that you are going to deal with at least two to four times. First and foremost this teaching will only be effective if you are willing to be honest with yourself. When you are honest in your desire to understand your need God will respond to you.

Don't fall into the trap like many believers who think they can lie to God in the way they answer these questions. When your sin is exposed to the light of God's truth and His presence, then you will find that the power of sin will be broken in your life. It's hard to overcome a sin and its power over you when it is hidden from God's light in the recesses of your life. There it is protected by your excuses and lies to yourself about you being helpless in being able to deal with the sin, or that it has too strong a hold on you, or you've been doing it too long to change. Now walk in truth as you use the truth of the following chapters to examine your life.

1. John 15
2. John 17
3. Romans 6
4. Romans 8
5. Romans 13 & 14
6. 1 Corinthians 13
7. 2 Corinthians 13:11
8. Galatians 5 & 6
9. Ephesians 4 & 5

10. Philippians 4
11. Colossians 3
12. James 4
13. 1 Peter 1
14. 2 Peter 1
15. 1 John 1-2 & 4
16. Psalm 139 & 147

Section Four: Self-Examination Questions
This last part of this self-examination exercise is a list of questions I came up with that helps you make course correction in specific areas. Some are based on biblical teachings, and the others on biblical principles. Some are based on common sense and experience. In doing this exercise, just choose one section to do at a sitting.

Complete one section a week or one a month. If you do it all the time it can become so commonplace that you don't take it seriously. Make your self-examination meaningful. Prepare your heart with prayer so you can more fully yield your will to God. Humble your heart and mind to God in that time of prayer. Refuse to defend those thoughts that justify your actions. Ask God to help you identify the areas you need to change in order to improve your life so you can have a closer walk with God.

How to implement the self-examination questions:
1. How have you specifically failed in the area questioned?
2. What specifically will you do to correct the problem?
3. Write down the changes you decide to make. Keep a journal that you can review on occasion to see how you are progressing.
4. Give yourself a time frame to start fulfilling your promise to God. Usually it should start the week you consider them. Be intentional and choose to carry out your actions for they may not feel natural at first. Allow yourself to fail several times before you get it right.
5. Some of these you can start immediately, and some can't take place until you are in a situation in which you can change your actions.
6. Review your commitments weekly to see how you have been doing.
7. What will change look like? The more specific and realistic you are in your thinking the better you can tell if you are progressing.

### Self Examination Questions
By Rev. Jim Olah

## Use of Time
*Am I spending too much time on the computer? - Watching TV?
*Do the books I read put sinful thoughts in my mind?

*Are the programs I watch on TV good for my spiritual life?

*Why do I think I need to watch TV so much? What could I do instead?

*Do I select videos or movies that are a negative impact to me spiritually?

*Why do I think I need to watch portrayals of negative, immoral or violent things that advance a wrong worldview? Does it devalue life or relationships?

*What makes the evil I watch on TV or in movies acceptable entertainment?

*What can I do to make my time count more for God? For spiritual growth? Learning the Bible?

*What can I do to reach my neighborhood for the Lord?

*Do I need to spend more time doing things with my spouse or family?

*Do I make time for personal spiritual involvement in prayer and Bible study?

*How can I make my time count for God, the church, the kingdom of God?

## Family

*Do I treat family members with respect?

*Am I showing genuine interest in family members? In church members?

*What grudges do I need to forgive family members?

*Do I show one face at home to my family and another face at church? (It's show time!)

*What are ways I can promote family unity instead of destroying it?

*Do I follow through on discipline with my children? Make them do their chores? Teach them to accept responsibility? Am I lax on my discipline with my children? Do I recognize poor discipline of my children as sin?

*Am I encouraging of the good that is in their life? Do I say such things as, "I admire the way you..." "I think you are good at..."

*Do I tell family members that I love them? Do I say it more than show it?

*With what kind of tone do I speak to my spouse or children?

*Does correction of my children discourage them or help them?

## My Spiritual Life

*Do I anticipate that God will work in your life today?

*Am I living by faith?

*Have I been reading my Bible in a thoughtful, contemplative way, or have I just been fulfilling my duty?

*Am I regularly applying what I've learned from my daily Bible reading to my daily life?

*Have my prayer requests been biblical? Have they been concerned with accomplishing God's will? Am I seeking to pray in fresh ways or am I always saying the same thing and using the same platitudes?

*Has my prayer life been a list of requests to God, or do I talk with God and fellowship with Him? Do I pray like I'm actually talking with a sentient being?

*Have I been singing to God during worship at church?

*Do I think about God and my faith when I sing?

*Is the music I listen to honoring God, or does my music endorse anti-god ways and values?

*Have I been coming to Church expecting to be entertained, or have I been worshipping with my singing and really talking to God in prayer?

*Have I been looking for ways to apply the pastor's sermons to my everyday life?

*Have I thought about what was taught on Sunday during the week?

*Have I been making excuses of not getting involved in a small group?

*Have I allowed fear to prevent me from praying in public?

*Am I afraid to pray regularly or publicly? Why?

*The excuse I use to not be faithful to the services of my church is...

*Instead of making excuses of avoiding church services I will...

*Have I taken seriously my responsibility to learn the Bible?

*Do I have a proper commitment to memorizing Bible passages so that I can become stronger in my faith?

*Am I taking seriously my duty to learn how to present the Gospel and learn what it is?

*What do I need to learn to become proficient in presenting the gospel?

*Does God want me to go on a short term mission trip?

*When we walk we throw ourselves off balance and the other foot comes automatically to catch us to keep us balanced and able to progress toward a goal. Do you know how to walk in the Spirit? Galatians 5:16-18

*We quench the spirit when we say no to his promptings. 1 Thessalonians 5:19 says "quench not the Spirit". How have you been quenching the Spirit? Or putting his fire out in your life?

## Morals

*Have I been viewing porn?

*Am I excusing my involvement in viewing porn?

*Have I come to a place where porn has an addictive hold on my life? (*Be honest with this and don't excuse any of it.*)

*What do I think God thinks of me watching porn? (Matt 5:27-28)

*Have I confessed my sin of my involvement in pornography?

*Am I involved in any inappropriate situations with the opposite sex? If so, how will I avoid it from now on?

*What is wrong with porn? How does porn affect my relationship with my spouse? Do I think porn hurts my spouse?

*Am I willing to turn my eyes away when I recognize a situation in which I will lust?

*Have I taken advantage of the opposite sex by seeking to seduce them into inappropriate actions?

*Is my manner of dress seductive? Too revealing? Properly modest?

 *Do I purposely dress in a manner to cause men to lust in what I reveal of my body?

*Do I take modesty into consideration in the way I dress?

*Do I steal from work?

*Has my character been established by truth?

*What excuses do I use to justify my lying?

*What lies do I need to stop telling?

## Communication

*Are the words of my mouth honorable to God?

*Do I excuse telling or listening to dirty jokes?

*Am I using God's name in vain, or in profanity in anyway?

*Do I curse, or use vulgarity?

 *Have I lied to anyone lately? Do I need to correct that lie with a person? Ask their forgiveness? Set the record straight?

 *Do I purposely exaggerate?

 *Do I admit when I am wrong?

*Am I communicating my true feelings and thoughts, or am I allowing lies and half-truths to shape my relationships with others? With my spouse?

*Do I keep my spouse informed about what is important in my life?

*Does my spouse know the struggles I am having in my life?

*Am I honest with my parents in what is going on in my life?

*Am I honest when my parents ask me where I have been?

*Do I talk *to* people or *with* people?

 *Are my children defensive when I speak to them or can I carry on a good conversation?

*Am I concerned enough about others to listen to what they have to say? Do I listen to what a person is saying, or do I plan out how I am going to respond? What's wrong when I mentally plan what I am going to say instead of fully listening to the other?

*Do I show I am listening by asking relevant questions about the topic of conversation? Am I concerned about what they are saying?

*Do I monopolize the conversation when talking with someone?

*Do I talk too much? Am I so taken up in what I have to say that I don't listen to others?

*Do I yell at my children too much? Do I belittle my children, or do I build them up in my communication with them? Is my communication with them positive or negative? Uplifting or demeaning? Loving or hateful?

*Have I been expressing appreciation, praise, or thanks to those around me on a regular basis?

## Self Control

*Am I able to control my responses to people? (I.e. not responding in anger, sarcasm, put-downs, undue emotion)

*How am I handling my weight problem? Am I over-eating? Under exercising? What excuse am I making for being overweight? What is the weak area I have the most difficulty facing in dealing with my weight?

*Am I keeping my house/room clean?

*Have I been handling my debt? Am I out of control? Do I have a plan to get out of debt?

*Do I get to appointments on time?

*Do I use my time wisely?

*Am I complaining, complimenting, or appreciating others?

*Does the way I drive indicate that I am not willing to control myself?

*In what way does my thought life indicate that I do not have self-control?

*Do I fanaticize about inappropriate situations with others?

*Am I taking time to contemplate God' spiritual issues in my life?

*Does the amount of time I spend watching TV or are on computer reflect that I have self control?

## Money - Tithing

*Have I used money inappropriately? Have I been spending God's money for self?

*Do I recognize that everything I have belongs to God?

*Have I been making excuses not to tithe?

*Have I been faithful in giving/tithing to my Church? Have I allowed fear that God might not provide for my need to keep me from tithing?

*Am I guilty of the sin of thinking that money will make me happy?

*Have I mishandled money to the point where I am in more debt than I can handle?

*Am I using money to seek happiness or control others?

*Is gambling becoming an addiction I have to do regularly?

*Do I trust more in the lottery than God to provide my needs?

*Has gambling become such a pull in my life that I don't focus enough on God and His provision?

*Do I excuse the sin of refusing to tithe by thinking that if I win big at gambling then I'll give a large amount to the church?

*Do I consider my refusal to tithe now as robbing God? (Malachi 3:8)

*Am I too overextended that I feel there is no way out?

*Do I think my amount of debt excuses me from my duty to God in the area of tithing?

*Is the reason I am not tithing because I don't think I can trust God to meet my needs?

*Am I a good steward of my finances by using a budget, and living in my means? If not, why not? Why have I not taken control of my budget?

*If I can't trust God in my finances can I trust Him to guide my life?

*If I don't obey God in the area of tithing am I also disobeying Him in other areas?

*Have I ever considered my lack of tithing a declaration that I don't love God as I should? (John 14:15)

## Thought Life

*What kinds of thoughts dominate my thought life? Does this need to change?

*Do I spend so much time daydreaming that I don't focus on reality?

*Do I fantasize about revenge? Hatred? Lust? Greed? Materialism? Wanting things? Being popular? Gaining power over people?

*Why am I allowing fear rather than the Holy Spirit control me?

*Is my thinking honest and clean in God's sight?

*In evening or morning when lying in bed, are my thoughts dwelling on good things? How should this change? On what am I going to focus my thoughts?

*Are my thoughts pure?

*Have I worried or been over-anxious about things about which I have no control?

*Do I fret? Do I complain about a lot of things? Does worry have me in bondage?

*How does my worry take my focus off God and His ability to help me?

*Have I learned how to meditate on Scripture? Memorize Scripture?

*Have I learned how to allow the peace of God to control my thought life?

*Is my mind in turmoil, or do I have peace of mind?

## Spiritual Life

*Why am I afraid to walk by faith?

*Why am I afraid to be sold out to God?

*Why do I think God can't be trusted with my children? With my job? With my reputation?

*Do I really think that God has my best interest in mind?

*Am I able to fully trust God to provide for me or help me in any situation in life?

*Does God want me to get involved in some ministry at the Church?

*If I had to choose to be involved in one area of ministry what would it be? Am I involved? If not, why?

*Does God want me to witness to someone specific?

*Who in my sphere of friends is not saved? What can I do to reach them for the Lord?

*Are the sins I was struggling with last year the same ones as this year?

*Have I experienced victory over particular sins? Have I praised God for my victory?

*Do I have cause to rejoice, or do I need to regroup over my spiritual progress?

*Am I applying Scripture to my daily life or just living life by my own authority?

*Am I seeking to know God better each day and because of each situation?

*Do I believe will set right the wrongs people do for me?

*Am I forgiving everyone as I ought? Am I forgiving everyone?

## Children, Young People

*Do I consistently show respect for my parents and their authority?

*Do I honor my parents?

*Do I argue with my parents over most things? Can I argue and still respect them?

*Why do I think it is all right to not treat my parents with respect when I answer them?

*Do I yell at them to get my way?

*Do I criticize my parents by calling them mean, or saying unkind things when they don't let me have my own way?

*Have I been obeying my parents?

*What do I think is motivating my parents when they deny my request? Are they out for vengeance, or do they really have my best interest in mind?

*Did I ask forgiveness for the wrong I did or the thoughtless words I said?

*Have I been treating my brothers/sisters properly?

*Have I been irritating my brothers/sisters on purpose? Have I asked their forgiveness?

*What can I do to better get along with my brothers/sisters?

*Have I been doing my chores at home? Without being told? Without complaining?

*Have I been doing my best at school?

*Have I been honoring God in the way I have been using my intelligence and learning at school?

*Have I been telling people at school about the Lord? Have I invited anyone to church?

*Have I been giving my teacher a difficult time?

*Have I been disrespecting my teacher?

*Would my school work be acceptable to God if I showed it to Him? Does my school work show that I am working up to my given ability?

*Have I taken my school tests honestly? Have I prepared for them adequately?

*Have I done my assignments to the best of my ability?

*Have I been dishonest by cheating on tests or copying someone else's homework?

**Parents**

*Do I yell at my children instead of talking with them?

*Do I constantly criticize my children without giving them praise?

*Do I keep my word with my children to do things with them?

*Am I active in discipling my children?

*Do I ask their forgiveness when I have not spoken to them with the right tone of voice? Or disciplined them unfairly before I knew the facts?

*Do I train my children in spiritual things?

*Do I model a good Christian example in the way I handle life and its difficulties?

*Do I train my children how to use money and establish a budget?

*Do I show my children how to love by loving my spouse?

*Do I exasperate my children by making unfair demands on them?

*Do I humiliate them when I discipline them?

*Do I yell at them for the little accidents that I excuse in myself, e.g. knocking over a glass of milk?

*Do they feel safe to ask questions and know I will do my best to answer them?

*Do I treat my children like I would like my parents to have treated me?

*Do I encourage my children? Do I show them appreciation?

*Do I build them up for the good they do?

*Do my children have freedom to fail without being humiliated by me?

*Do I have a plan for the good morals and ethics I want developed in them?

*Do I take them to church weekly?

**Divorced and your Ex**

*Am I treating my Ex with respect or am I tearing them down at strategic opportunities?

*Am I involving my children in a power struggle with my Ex?

*Am I paying my child support regularly?

*Do I choose to not be understanding with my Ex?

*Do I seek to get information out of my children to use against my Ex?

*Am I working with my Ex to make sure the children are up on their homework, grades and school attendance?

*Do I take advantage of my Ex by not providing clothing and toys at my home, or not taking it back when the children return?

*Am I doing my part to remain on friendly terms with my Ex?

*Do I speak to my Ex in a civil manner?

*Do I intentionally do things to irritate my Ex?

*Am I provoking a power struggle with my Ex?

*Am I purposely unreasonable with my EX?

*Have I been able to let go of the pain he or she caused me?

*Am I willing to trust God's command enough to personally forgive my Ex fully and totally?
*Do I pray for my Ex and their needs?
*Am I faithful in being on time with child transfers?
*Do I keep my word with my children? If I say I'm going to be there to get them for something special, can they always count on me?
*If I can't be there for a meeting do I call and let them know?
*Do I pray for my children regularly?
*Do I make my children take sides between me and my Ex?
*Do I bad-mouth my Ex in front of my children?
*Do I work with my Ex to make sure common discipline rules are in place for the children?
*Am I still seeking to keep up my children's spiritually involved in the church?

**Senior Adults**
*Do I trust God to meet my needs?
*Am I leaving a good example for my children and grandchildren to follow?
*Have I made things right that hurt my children as I raised them?
*Are there issues that I need to ask their forgiveness for the specific wrongs I did to them or the wrong way I acted?
*Have I told my children that I love them and how important they are to me? Have I told them I am proud of them? Have I given my children my blessing in what they are doing? Have I praised the good things I see in them for how they turned out?
*Do I think everyone owes me, or do I still serve others with a sweet spirit?
*Is my spirit bitter or sweet?
*Have I given up serving the Lord because I'm too old?
*Are there some people that I could reach for Christ?
*Who are some young people I could mentor or encourage?

**Employee**
*Have I been giving my employer my best?
*Have I been a good testimony for God?
*Have I been taking things from work that don't belong to me?
*Do people know I am a Christian and that God is important to me?
*Would the quality of work I am doing be pleasing to God if He were to inspect it?
*Am I talking too much during work time instead of doing my work?
*Am I a complainer at work?
*Do I make the work place a pleasant or a miserable place for others?
*Do I honor my employer by using my time fully for him?
*Am I doing my best to make my boss a success?

*Do I work to serve the Lord or am I just there for a pay check?
*Do I recognize that it honors God to do my best at work?

**Church attender**
*Do I attend church weekly?
*Do I go with the attitude that I want to learn something? That I want to worship God?
*Do I find myself judging others and their motives?
*Do I view the pastor as a representative of God who has a message for me?
*Do I honor the position of the pastor that if he makes a decision to take the church in a new direction that I seek to support him instead of hindering him?
*Do I listen to the sermon with the motivation to learn something that I can incorporate into my life?
*Do I go to church as a judge (judge the quality of the sermon, the kind of music, and the actions of teens)?
*Do I go to church to serve others?
*Am I actively using my spiritual gift at church?
*Do I support my church as I should with serving, giving, being friendly to others and welcoming guests?
*Do I regularly invite people to church?
*Do I support the extra activities of the church beyond Sunday service?
*If your church has small groups, are you involved?
*What kind of service would you like to be involved in at the church?
*Do you greet people around you each week at church?
*Do you seek to make guest feel comfortable by talking with them?
*Do you encourage the children and teens? Are you friendly with them?
*Do you support people in the church whose spouse or family member died, by attending the wake or funeral, or doing something for the family?
*Do I look at church as a place to be served or a place to serve?
*Do I look at church as merely a means to do my duty to God, or do I see church as an opportunity to get to know God better and worship corporately with fellow believers?
*Do I worship God or just go through the motions?

These are questions I developed to help people more effectively examine their self for communion. It is a good exercise for the Christian to evaluate where their weaknesses are so they can effect change.

© Jim Olah: jso46@hotmail.com. Written 2/25/02. Revised 1/07; 2/11, 5/12

69

# Chapter 11 – Forgiving as a Christian

One of the important issues that become very difficult for many of us to face is that of forgiving those who have hurt, offended, betrayed, hated, and forsaken us or any number of other offensive things. Jesus tells us that we must forgive people. Paul tells us that we are to forgive others in the same way we have been forgiven by God. Following the section that presents scripture passages that call us to forgive, I then offer you a sample prayer that will help you focus on the issues of forgiveness that you need to address.

I offer you these passages of scripture that call us to forgive. I do so without commentary. Allow the passages to speak to you. As hard as forgiveness is, God still requires us to do it. Often we don't forgive because that person really hurt us and we think that if we forgive them they are getting off scot-free. God doesn't say that we are to forgive because it is easy; He is saying that we need to forgive because He calls us to. It is not our job to take vengeance and set things right, it is His. What we need to keep in mind is that we forgive because God has forgiven us so much. Jesus makes this so clear in Luke 7:36-50.

Scriptures to read and memorize on forgiveness
1. Eph 4:30-32 *"And do not grieve the Holy Spirit of God, with whom you were sealed for the day of redemption. Get rid of all bitterness, rage and anger, brawling and slander, along with every form of malice. Be kind and compassionate to one another, forgiving each other, just as in Christ God forgave you."*

2. Col. 3:13 *"Bear with each other and forgive whatever grievances you may have against one another. Forgive as the Lord forgave you."*

3. Mat. 6:14-15 *"For if you forgive men when they sin against you, your heavenly Father will also forgive you. But if you do not forgive men their sins, your Father will not forgive your sins."*

4. Luke 23:34 *"Jesus said, 'Father, forgive them, for they do not know what they are doing...'"*

5. Mat 18:32-35 *"Then the master called the servant in.' You wicked servant,' he said, 'I canceled all that debt of yours because you begged me to. Shouldn't you have had mercy on your fellow servant just as I had on you?' In anger his master turned him over to the jailers to be tortured, until he should pay back all he owed. This is how my heavenly Father will treat each of you unless you forgive your brother from your heart."*

6. Matthew 18:21-22 *"Then Peter came and said to him, 'Lord, how often shall my brother sin against me, and I forgive him? Until seven times?' Jesus said to him, 'I don't tell you until seven times, but, until seventy times seven.'"*

I preached a sermon on the Matthew 6 passage that addressed the importance of forgiveness. Afterwards one of the people came up to me and said that I just didn't understand why she had a right to not forgive the person who had hurt her. She thought that because she was hurt so bad and that it was difficult for her to forgive, this exempted her from doing it. What she failed to realize is that it was not my idea that she had to forgive, it was commanded by Jesus. In Matthew 6:14-15 Jesus said we have to forgive. If we value God's forgiveness of us, then we need to be serious about forgiving others.

How many times do you sin against God? Keep in mind God's definitions of sin given us in the Bible. You sin when you don't choose to do right when you have opportunity, when you don't walk by faith, when you don't pray about everything, when you live in fear, when you hate, and when you don't love. Are your thoughts always pure? Are your motives holy? Do you always tell the truth? Has a day gone by without lust in some form? You can sin in word, thought and deed. You sin by doing wrong and by omitting the good God calls all people to do. Are you starting to see that we sin a lot more than we recognize?

Consider this little number game about your sins. If you only committed three sins a day, then in a year you would be responsible for offending God 1000 times. If you are 32 years old, that would be 32,000 sins. God forgives every one of your sins fully and freely. If truth be told we fail God many more times than that a day. Maybe we sin 20 or 50 times a day or more. Thirty sins a day would make 18,250 sins added to our account before God each year. Multiply that times 32 years, and you have over a half a million sins (584,000) against you.

Each time you sinned God has been offended by you, and each time you need His forgiveness. Christians have been forgiven by God fully and freely every time. Non-believers still have those sins against their account. God says "Now I want you to forgive your offenders as fully and freely as I forgive you." It is when we fail to recognize how much we have offended God that we tend to become unforgiving toward others. (Luke 7:47) *"Therefore I tell you, her sins, which are many, are forgiven, for she loved much. But to whom little is forgiven, the same loves little."* (Read the whole account on your own.)

As long as you refuse to forgive, that person holds you in bondage. Your mind cannot let go of the hurt and you think of ways to get even. Release them through forgiveness and set yourself free.

Are you ready to become free from your enslavement to your bitterness by choosing to totally forgiven the person or persons who hurt or offended you? Against whom are you holding a grudge that you are unwilling to forgive? What kind of excuses are you using to prevent you from being obedient to God? What excuse are you using to hold on to your "right" to withhold forgiveness? Let this prayer be a pattern for you to follow in forgiving your offender.

## Prayer of Forgiveness

*"Lord, I have been hurt by _____ and you know the situation. I've been replaying that hurt for years, and I know all the ways I would like to hurt this person or take revenge on him, or ruin his reputation. Lord, it has consumed me. My unforgiveness has had a choke hold on the person's neck. Now, in obedience to your word, I give this hurt over to you, and I forgive this person. Lord, vengeance is yours, it is yours to repay in your time and in your way. I am now willing to trust this hurt into your authority. I have committed so many sins and been forgiven more sins that I have done against you than that person or any other could ever have done to me. In spite of all that, you have forgiven me, and I have held on to my right to hold a grudge and not forgive that person.*

*Forgive me for not taking the teaching of your word on forgiveness seriously. I ask you to work in that person's life in a gracious way so he won't be offensive to others. If he is not saved, I ask that he will come to faith in Christ. If he is saved, he is my brother in Christ, and I ask that you would draw him into a right relationship with You, and that he would become more holy. Right now I give up my vindictiveness, and I place the results in your just hands. Even as I want your blessing in my life after I am forgiven by You, I ask You to bless _____. Lord, teach me your ways, and I commit myself to become more like your Son in the way I respond to those who hurt and offend me. In Jesus's name I pray. Amen"*

Why Forgiving is Important to You

Forgiveness is just as much for you as it is the other person. As long as you refuse to forgive that person you are out of fellowship with God. That is the meaning in Matthew 6 when Jesus said if you won't forgive neither will your father in heaven forgive you. How can He give you His full blessing when you are choosing to live in bondage to the sin of hatred or vengeance? Refusing to forgive is in direct violation of the teaching of God's word. It takes on a responsibility that is God's alone.

Forgiving helps you to trust in God. Forgiving recognizes and believes that God will bring about proper vengeance, whether it is in this life or the next. You live by faith when you believe that He will live out His holy and righteous nature. Being willing to forgive demonstrates that you have confidence in the fact that He is just. It recognizes that the Judge of all the earth shall do right by you and with the offender. When we fail to forgive, we aren't taking our responsibilities to God seriously. We think our actions of revenge against a person will carry out justice better than God will.

Forgiveness is an exercise in obedience.
1. Are we willing to trust God and believe God?
2. Are we willing to allow God to fight our battles?
3. Are we willing to believe that God has a plan and purpose for us as well as the offender?
4. Are we willing to learn how to put God's word into practice as a result of our hurts?
5. Are we willing to see that God's word really works better than our own preconceived earthly ideas?

Forgiving is not just important, it is expected of you if you want to please God, have fellowship with Him and to grow in your faith. You aren't fully obedient to God's word if you aren't forgiving your offender. 1 John 4:20 says: *"If a man says, 'I love God,' and hates his brother, he is a liar; for he who doesn't love his brother whom he has seen, how can he love God whom he has not seen?"* Forgiving is a way of expressing love to your brother or sister in Christ. Of course you need to forgive unsaved people or ask forgiveness, whichever the need is.

Here is one last point to consider. When someone offends you sometimes you may have caused it. Even if it is only 10% your fault, you need to deal with your sin. We tend to focus on the hurt the other person did to us and fail to see our own wrong in the whole situation. We understand our motivation of what we did, and so we justify it as acceptable and can only see the wrong the other has done. That is what Matthew 7:1-6 addresses. Be willing to see your own fault and your own guilt and deal with it before you pull the telephone pole out of your offender's eye. Examine your own attitudes, actions and words. When it comes to words, consider also the way you responded with the tone of your voice, because that can set some people off as well. Examine yourself in God's presence and listen to the Holy Spirit. If something comes to your mind, don't justify it; own up to it and confess it as sin. Get right with God before you go on to make it right with your offender.

I have found that when I have been offended by people, I usually ask God what He wants me to learn from this and how He wants me to represent Him as I go to the offending party. We must realize that in the way we deal with every situation, we are God's servant carrying out His will. We are his representative. That helps us have a better attitude and motivation in addressing the issue with the person.

**Excellent resource: TOTAL FORGIVENESS --** by Kendall, R.T, published by Charisma House, also a Kindle Book

# Chapter 12 - Bible Study: Food for Growth

Just as food is important to life so is spiritual food to the Christian life. The new believer needs to develop the ability to feed on the word of God. The mature Christian needs to maintain this spiritual diet. When Jesus was being tempted by the Devil in the wilderness He was tempted to turn the stones into bread. But his reply told Satan that there is something more important than food. "It is written, *'Man shall not live by bread alone, but by every word that proceeds out of the mouth of God.'*" (Matthew 4:4) The word of God is essential to spiritual growth.

Watch that you don't buy into ideas that exempt you from regular Bible reading and study. Those excuses come in such forms as: "I'm too busy." "I just don't get anything out of it most of the time." "It's too hard for me to comprehend." "I'm not a reader." "Certainly God doesn't expect me to do it every day." Be aware of how your old nature seeks to find ways to exempt you from spending time in God's Word.

As you begin your journey into your new life, remember that you must eat along the way, and your spiritual food is the Word of God. Your goal is not just to read it, but understand it and apply it to your life. Can you imagine sitting at a meal and after you put each fork of food into your mouth you spit it out. After a big meal you would say, "I ate a lot but I'm still very hungry." What kind of fool does that? But that is what believers often do with God's word. They hurry through reading it and spit it out and go their way without any thought of how it should affect their life that day. When you eat, you must put the food in your mouth. Chew on it for a while and swallow it into your being. Allow it to give you nutrition to live out your faith that day as you recall it and claim its authority in your life. Your goal is to understand God and His ways so you can live out your new life in this foreign land called earth.

Moses declared the importance of the Word of God to the believer in Deuteronomy 32:46-47b "*Set your heart to all the words which I testify to you this day, which you shall command your children to observe to do, all the words of this law. For it is no vain thing for you; because it is your life...*" This goes beyond a casual reading or understanding of God's Word. He said "*Set your heart to all the words...*" It becomes the standard by which you judge and evaluate life as well as what directs your life and establishes your priorities. Secondly He said "*it is no vain thing for you because it is your life...*" The Word of God is what life is about, that is why it is to be so important. Make the word of God the same priority to your spiritual life as food is to your physical life. The normal person would not even consider missing several meals in a row. That priority for feeding on God's word needs to be established for our spiritual life as well.

The following actions and commitments can help you increase your Bible knowledge and understandings:

*Make a commitment to God.* Declare your commitment to get to know His word in an experientially and practical way. Intentionally chose to have God's Word affect every area of your life and priorities. Look for ways to apply the teaching of God's word to your life. What did I read today or recently that I can apply to today? How do we put God's word into action?

*Attend a Bible-believing Church.* Make sure you attend Church regularly where the Bible is valued and faithfully taught. Do they believe and teach what is presented in chapter one that presents our belief in the Bible? Look for a church that preaches through whole books of the Bible. The pastor will preach verse by verse, paragraph by paragraph, giving you the background and meaning of words and the passage, helping you understand how to apply it to your life.

*Listen to good speakers on Christian radio.* There are a lot of good speakers and Bible teachers on Christian radio. Find a good station in your area and listen when you drive. Some of these programs also offer free podcasts of their programs that you can listen to at your convenience. They are usually free.

*Read good books.* Christianity has a plethora of good books that deal with specific topics. They apply the Word of God to issues that are of concern to you. Some deal with addictions, as well as family matters, how to pray, how do deal with suffering, and how to serve the Lord or reach out to the community. Good books are really like good sermons that help you apply God's word to specific areas of your life. There are many good Christian fiction books that apply the teachings of Scripture to everyday life. Bodie and Brock Thoene have written an excellent series on the time of Christ called A.D. Chronicles. I really enjoyed this series and it taught me a lot about what life was like in the first century. There are many other good authors who can teach Christian truth through their stories.

*Read the Bible.* Some people like to read through the Bible in a year. That's about three chapters a day. There are a lot of reading guides out there to help you. I've never read through the Bible in a year, but some people like to do it. I've read through the Bible several times, but it will usually take me two to three years. I go at a comfortable speed and will sometimes camp out on a passage or book. Listening to the Bible being read is also good. It helps you follow the context better. Have a regular reading plan where you read at least a chapter a day at a regular time. My time is at the breakfast table. I read the Bible as I eat breakfast. I will read five to six days a week. What I want to emphasize is that you have an appointed time to read. That way if you miss your scheduled time you will know that you missed your appointment with God. It is amazing how God leads you to the exact scripture you need as you are dealing with specific problems in your life. You will find that exciting.

As you read your Bible, always go with an inquiring mind. Ask questions that will help you understand the text and help you apply the teaching to your life.

Here is a list of questions to keep on your mind as you read. You might want to type this up and make it into a bookmark that you use in your Bible.

As you study your Bible ask yourself if there is:
1. A sin I should avoid.
2. A promise I can claim.
3. A command for me to obey.
4. A blessing I can enjoy.
5. A teaching to guide my Christian life.
6. A victory for me to win.
7. An important teaching about God, the Lord Jesus, the Holy Spirit, Satan, man.
8. A truth that has stood out to me.

*Get a good study Bible.* You will find that a study Bible will be a good resource to expand your understanding. In a study Bible you will find notes explaining the meaning of key passages. Cross references indicate other Bible passages that deal with the same topic or show you where the quote is found in other places in the Bible. Concordances at the back will help you find passages by using key words. Some have a dictionary that defines key people, events, places and teachings of the Bible. Each study Bible offers different kinds of resources. Even if you have a study Bible on your computer, lap top, or tablet, it is nice having something you can physically refer to and even use in Church or with other people. There are so many study Bible's available I don't know them all. Some of the ones with which I am familiar are: Ryrie Study Bible, MacArthur Study Bible, NIV Study Bible, ESV study Bible. If you want a study Bible that helps you understand the words in their original language there is the Hebrew-Greek Key Word Study Bible- by Spiros Zodhiates. It is in both KJV and NASV. (That is the King James Version and New American Standard Version.) Ask your pastor or a mature believer what they would recommend.

*Use Devotion Guides.* Some people like devotion guides to help them get into the Bible daily. It's like having someone share their insights about a passage of scripture each day. One of the popular devotion guides is Our Daily Bread. It offers a passage from the Bible each day and then a comment about some portion of your Bible reading. You can read it on line or order a free copy to come to your home four times a year (http://odb.org/). There are also other books that offer daily or study guides to help you.

*Variety is the spice of life.* Make sure you put variety into your Bible study or devotion time. Read through the Bible one year. Get involved in an in-depth book study for several months (described below.). Use a book like Purpose Driven Life by Rick Warren, or Love Dare. My wife used to like to go through a study book by Beth Moore or some other person as part of her devotions. Take a month and memorize a chapter of the Bible. Read through the Bible in a month. Spend an hour a day, every day, and read as much as you can. Louie was a friend who would get off work at midnight and read until 7 or 8 the next morning. He was in love with God and His word. Spend a week or month in extensive reading instead of going on the computer or watching TV. Get in the habit of writing down thoughts and ideas as you read or study. Keep a note pad with your Bible so you can record that which grabs you. Use a hymn book to sing praise to God when you are so led. Some creative people might want to write songs from the scripture that has touched them. What I'm saying by all of this is, recognize that variety in the way you do devotions is good. Don't allow your devotions to be a dry, boring habit that you do just because you have to. Devotions should be like a relationship in that you discover new things and do new things together. Keep this time fresh and interesting because it is in times like this that you are more likely to learn and meet God in fresh ways.

Check out some of these sites:
http://www.backtothebible.org/devotions.html
http://www.crosswalk.com/devotionals/ This place offers websites of nationally known preachers.
http://www.tyndale.com/20_Bibles/devotionals.php You can sign up for a variety of devotions.
http://www.cbhministries.org/ForKids/KeysforKids/ReadListen.aspx This is a great place for children's daily devotions. We used these with our children and they really relate well to kids.

## Do an in-depth study on your own

I have challenged people to spend several months on one book of the Bible to master it. You can only pick up so much by reading a passage. If you take a 4-6 chapter book of the Bible and spend several months studying it and noticing the detail, you will come away having mastered that book. The advantage of doing this is that when you read or study other books of the Bible you will find much of what you learned relating to your in-depth study. It enhances your understanding on different levels and helps you get a more complete picture of the teaching of the Bible.

What follows is the guide that I have made available to those who have taken this challenge and done the study. I challenge you to do at least one in-depth study to help you experience the benefit of such an exercise. Even though it takes a lot of work you will never regret what you glean from your study.

# The Bible Study Project

A. *Choose a short book* from the New Testament, 4-6 chapters. (John 13-17, Galatians, Philippians, Ephesians, Colossians, 1 or 2 Thessalonians, 1 or 2 Timothy, James, 1 Peter, 1 John)

B. *Read the book 10 times.* Read with an inquisitive mind. Each time you read through, notice the development of the major points. What seems important? What is being emphasized? How is the theme tied together? What are key words that are used repeatedly? What lessons are specifically noted? Such reading requires thought on your part. Make sure you record your thoughts, questions and observations as you read. Use various translations to get a different perspective (http://www.biblegateway.com/). This site has over 20 different versions or translations of the Bible.( http://www.biblestudytools.com/bible-versions/) also offers Bible versions and Bible study tools.)

C. *Outline the book.* You can make this simple or detailed. Don't copy it from some other source. Develop the outline yourself. Outlining forces you to notice the various themes and how the book fits together.

D. *Notice the various teaching* used to get the truth across. What does this book teach about **God**? List the quality and the reference to each quality (Attributes God's standards, God's work, and qualities of God important to you). What does the book teach about Christian living, standing for the truth, opposing doctrinal error, etc?

E. *Pick out 10 important words* from each chapter and define them. Use a book that bases the explanation on the original language (Greek). (The Online Bible offers Bible versions to put on your computer as well as many study tools and language study tools. http://www.onlinebible.net/ Also see http://www.olivetree.com/ and http://www.e-sword.net/. Some of these have programs for your tablets and smart phones. Some of the modules are free, and some charge a fee. Learn to use these tools to help you get a better understanding of the passages. The Albert Barns and Jamieson, Fausset and Brown Commentaries are good free modules to add into the Bible software. A good Bible Study program that is expensive is "Logos". You get a good library but can spend from $250-$5000.00 for the various modules. Many pastors use this program for their studies. Quick Verse or Word Search is a reasonably priced Bible-study program offering excellent Bibles and resource books. A good one might go from $30-250.00. I use Logos, Quick Verse and Online Bible for my studies, and they are very helpful.

F.  *The power of observation.* Take your favorite passage from the book (no more than 3 verses) and make 35 observations about those verses. Write out your observations. What is this verse saying as well as what is it not saying? Observe what is significant to you. Don't stop working until you get 35 observations. Try to go beyond 35. Work on this for a week or two. Think about it often. The more you work to see what is there, the more you will observe, and the easier the observation will become with other passages. Here is an example of how you would go about this:

Titus 2:13 *"while we wait for the blessed hope--the glorious appearing of our great God and Savior, Jesus Christ,"* Here is a sample of some observations of this verse:

1.  "We" refers to a specific group of people. Which group?
2.  The appearing of Jesus for us is going to be glorious. Something worth seeing! Describe it.
3.  Our Savior is called God. God provided my redemption!
4.  We need to learn to wait for this event that is really great. What worthwhile thing will I do while I wait? How can I please God while I wait? How can I serve Him?
5.  The appearing (rapture), is not something that God assigns to an inferior being to carry out. God, Himself, will come for us.
6.  What is the difference between appearing and glorious appearing? Emphasis is added to help us recognize that it is something special. The best of what God is will be displayed.
7.  We have a hope. Hope is a confident expectation of good. How should that hope motivate and help me?
8.  The Blessed Hope is the appearing of Jesus Christ.

When you learn to notice details and facts in this exercise, the Bible will become more meaningful. The reason we miss so many blessings is because we do not pay attention to details and meaning of words. God knows how to pack details into His revelation. If we don't accurately know God's word, then how can we accurately live a godly life, make right choices, and properly understand God and His ways?

G.  *Read a commentary on the book.* Don't read a commentary until you have finished the above exercises. Get used to digging the truth out on your own. Let commentaries give you fuller meaning, background, and language expertise that you lack as well as their perspective of applying the passage. The purpose of commentaries is to explain the book. Some do so verse by verse, others paragraph by paragraph. Some thought by thought. Some explain the meaning of words, and others talk about how to understand the passage. Many make application. Are you starting to get the idea that commentaries actually do what I am having you do in this exercise? It takes work, but don't back down from the challenge. When you finish you will never regret doing this spiritually enlightening exercise.

H. *Identify a key paragraph* of at least 5 verses long, and write a short paper as if you were explaining it to someone who needed to understand this truth. Seek to explain the passage in your own words and apply its truths. Think of how you would teach this passage to a class, to a new Christian, or explain it to a friend. What is important in that passage? Why is it important to you? How can this passage help someone who wants to grow in their faith? What did the teaching of this passage clear up about life for you?

I. *Memorize at least three to fifteen verses* from the book you study. If you want a real challenge memorize a whole chapter or the whole book. There is no better way to pick up on the detail of the book. You might want to start by only memorizing a favorite chapter. If God challenges you to memorize a whole chapter or the whole book, then don't back down from this. It is possible. Have others listen to you so they can help you get detail straight. It can also encourage them. I memorized the book of 2 Timothy many years ago. My brother-in-law, Don memorized Philippians and 1 John. Memorization starts off with getting really familiar with a passage. Read it over and over. Write out verses five or ten times that you want to memorize. Make up memory verse cards. Place the verse on one side and the reference on the other. Take it with you and read it over 5-10 times every day for a month. You will know it before you realize it. When you memorize a verse you will find that God will then give you opportunity to use it in conversations with people and in discerning issues of life. "*Your word have I hid in my heart that I might not sin against you.*" (Psalm 119:11)

J. *After you are finished with your study, write a paragraph* or paper about the most significant lesson you learned, or make a list of the teachings that affected the way you view your life and that helped you. Completing this task of doing the intensive Bible Study on your own is a great accomplishment. In another paragraph, tell why you would recommend this to someone else.

K. *Write me an E-mail* and tell me about some of the things you have learned and appreciated from doing this exercise. I would be interested in hearing from those who have done this study. Also please share that review of this book on Amazon.

L. *Plan on taking at least 3-6 months with the project*, and there is nothing wrong with working on it for the whole year. Commit yourself to learning one book of the Bible. Select a time to do your study on a regular basis. You can either do this on a daily basis, or you can set aside one evening or morning each week to dedicated study time. An hour may seem like a long time until you get hooked on the benefit. You might want to start off with at least 15 - 30 minutes per session. It takes time to dig and learn. After being involved in this study for a while, step it up and block off a full hour to spend on your study once a month. In some of my studies I have spend whole days or several hours in the evening. I always came away invigorated.

You might want to type your notes on a computer or use a notebook to keep track of your research. Take time before and even during your studies to pray. Ask the Holy Spirit to open the eyes of your understanding (Ephesians 1:18) to the meaning and application of the Scriptures. Talk to God much about the meaning of the scriptures.

Jim Olah -12/8/98

Is this kind of study important? Let me tell you the story of my friend Richard Owen. Earlier in his life Richard had people telling him a lot of things about his faith that he didn't think was right. What he recognized was that these people were legalists. So he did an intensive study in the book of Galatians. He got a good grasp of the book and gained an understanding of how legalism works and how it enslaves people.

There are so many situations that we talk about with each other that Richard can easily relate back to Galatians. He talks intelligently about a person's view, and it reflects an accurate understanding of the Bible's teaching on legalism. I am always amazed at the insights he has on this topic. But that understanding did not come without work on his part. He has never regretted investing himself in this study, for it has affected his life in such a positive way. Since the 20 years I've known Richard, he is still getting a better grasp on this topic, because he is seeing how legalism plays out in people's lives. This outcome is because he developed a good foundation in God's word.

Let me encourage you to invest yourself into some serious study of God's word. In this way you will not be blown around by every wind of doctrine because of your ignorance (Ephesians 4:14)

# Chapter 13 - Never Forget Who You Are

You will face many battles in the journey, and you will experience times where, because of your failure, you will feel unimportant, unworthy and even a complete failure. During these times you need to read over the following list to remind yourself of who you are and what God did for you. These blessings, positions and advantages don't change on a whim like our emotions. They are firmly established in heaven and based on the authority of God's unchanging word. Let this section be a retreat for you when you feel defeated or worthless.

My prayer for you is what the Apostle Paul prayed for us in Ephesians 1:18-19a *"having the eyes of your hearts enlightened, that you may know what is the hope of his calling, and what are the riches of the glory of his inheritance in the saints, and what is the exceeding greatness of his power toward us who believe"*. When we know the hope of God's calling of us, it helps us have direction in life and keeps us stable through the roughest of problems and hurts. The part I want you to experience in this study is Paul's second request, which prays that you would understand from God's perspective how He values you as "the riches of his glorious inheritance in the saints". He considers you his glorious inheritance! When we belittle ourselves, feel inferior, feel inadequate, we fail to recognize our value and worth in God's eyes. That brings us to the last request. That you would have your eyes open to the great power that is available to overcome anything, and serve God in any way he calls you because of the power available to you in Christ. It is the same power that it took to resurrect Christ from the dead.

When you have an X-ray taken of you the insides of your body are shown. If you have a broken bone that is revealed. If there is a growth on some organ of your body it is shown for the doctor to see. These verses are like the X-ray machine. It shows parts of you that are not visible to the naked eye. These qualities that God provides for you at salvation are not felt, or obvious to you or others. God declares what He has made you and how He has blessed you in rich ways. I call these God's Benefit Package for the believer.

You are about to see a glimpse of the glorious riches of God's grace in our salvation. There are many who think salvation is simply a kick-start in the right direction, and we have to do the rest of the perfecting work. It's true we have to work on change, but notice the well-equipped salvation God lavishly bestowed on us at salvation. None of these things are earned, but are freely given to each one at the moment we are saved. Be amazed, be encouraged, and be overwhelmed at the goodness of God as you read what He has done for YOU. No one gets a discounted or scaled-down version of God's salvation, but each person has a fully loaded version. These benefits are all *yours* in Christ. You can never lose them. Don't allow anyone to cause you to think that you are in some way inferior in your salvation. Walk with confidence in your acceptance by God. Now let's look at your benefit package in salvation.

1.  *Every Believer is a* **member of the body of Christ** (1 Corinthians 12:13) "For in one Spirit we were all baptized into one body, whether Jews or Greeks, whether bond or free; and were all given to drink into one Spirit."

2.  Every Believer is a **member of the family of God**. (*John 1:12*) *"But as many as received him, to them he gave the right to become God's children, to those who believe in his name:"*

3.  Every Believer is a **son or daughter of God** (*Galatians 3:26*) *"For you are all children of God, through faith in Christ Jesus."*

4.  Every Believer is **adopted**.(*Galatians 4:4-6*) *"But when the fullness of the time came, God sent out his Son, born to a woman, born under the law, that he might redeem those who were under the law, that we might receive the adoption of children. And because you are children, God sent out the Spirit of his Son into your hearts, crying, 'Abba, Father!'"*The difference between being born into the family and being adopted is that birth brings you into the family. Adoption raises you to the level of an adult giving you the full rights and privileges as an adult in the family.

5.  Every Believer has been **cleansed by the blood of Jesus Christ**. (*Ephesians 1:7*) *"in whom we have our redemption through his blood, the forgiveness of our trespasses, according to the riches of his grace."*

6.  Every Believer has been fully **forgiven**. (*Colossians 1:14*) *"in whom we have our redemption, the forgiveness of our sins."*

7.  Every Believer has been **redeemed** from the slave market of sin and set free through the precious blood of Jesus. (*1 Peter 1:18-19*) *"knowing that you were redeemed, not with corruptible things, with silver or gold, from the useless way of life handed down from your fathers, but with precious blood, as of a faultless and pure lamb, the blood of Christ."*

8.  Every Believer has been **reconciled to God.** (*2* Corinthians *5:19-20*) *"...God was in Christ reconciling the world to himself, not reckoning to them their trespasses, and having committed to us the word of reconciliation."*

9.  Every Believer has been **regenerated**. Life and the divine nature have been imparted to each one. (*Titus 3:5*) *"not by works of righteousness,*

*which we did ourselves, but according to his mercy, he saved us, through the washing of regeneration and renewing by the Holy Spirit."*

10. Every Believer has been **made near** or brought close **to God** by the blood of Jesus. (*Ephesians 2:13*) *"But now in Christ Jesus you who once were far off are made near in the blood of Christ."* (To be brought near to God suggests that we were far off before, and now we are close in relationship to God.)

*11.* Every Believer has been **accepted in the beloved**. (*Ephesians 1:6*) *"to the praise of the glory of his grace, by which he freely bestowed favor on us in the Beloved."*

12. Every Believer is, right now, a **citizen of heaven**. (*Philippians 3:20*) *"For our citizenship is in heaven, from where we also wait for a Savior, the Lord Jesus Christ."*

*13.* Every Believer has been **justified** or declared absolutely righteous so he can be fully accepted by God. (*Romans 5:9*) *"Much more then, being now justified by his blood, we will be saved from God's wrath through him."*

*14.* Every Believer is a **royal priest**. (*1 Peter 2:9*) *"But you are a chosen race, a royal priesthood, a holy nation, a people for God's own possession, that you may proclaim the excellence of him who called you out of darkness into his marvelous light."*

*15.* Every Believer has been **chosen in Him before the foundation of the world**. (*Ephesians 1:4*) *"even as he chose us in him before the foundation of the world, that we would be holy and without blemish before him in love."*

*16.* Every Believer is already **seated in the heavenly realms in Christ Jesus.** (*Ephesians 1:3*) *"Blessed be the God and Father of our Lord Jesus Christ, who has blessed us with every spiritual blessing in the heavenly places in Christ."*

*17.* Every Believer possesses **everlasting life**. (*John 3:36*) *"One who believes in the Son has eternal life, but one who disobeys the Son won't see life, but the wrath of God remains on him." (John 6:47): "Most certainly, I tell you, he who believes in me has eternal life." (1 John 5:11-13) "The testimony is this that God gave to us eternal life, and this life is in his Son. He who has the Son has the life. He who doesn't have God's Son doesn't have the life. These things I have written to you who believe in the name of* *the Son of God, that you may know that you have eternal life, and that you may continue to believe in the name of the Son of God."*

18. Every Believer is a **saint.** (Romans *1:7) "to all who are in Rome, beloved of God, called to be saints: Grace to you and peace from God our Father and the Lord Jesus Christ."* A saint is one separated to God.

19. Every Believer has been **baptized into Christ**. (*Romans 6:3-5) "Or don't you know that all we who were baptized into Christ Jesus were baptized into his death? We were buried therefore with him through baptism to death that just like Christ was raised from the dead through the glory of the Father, so we also might walk in newness of life. For if we have become united with him in the likeness of his death, we will also be part of his resurrection." (1 Cor. 12:13) "For in one Spirit we were all baptized into one body, whether Jews or Greeks, whether bond or free; and were all given to drink into one Spirit."*

20. Every Believer is **free from Condemnation**. (*Romans 8:1) "There is therefore now no condemnation to them that are in Christ Jesus." (Romans 5:9) "Much more then, being now justified by his blood, shall we be saved from the wrath of God through him."* No guilt of sin hinders your relationship with God.

21. Every Believer is **inseparable from the Love of God**. (*Romans 8:38-39)* "For I am persuaded, that neither death, nor life, nor angels, nor principalities, nor things present, nor things to come, nor powers, nor height, nor depth, nor any other created thing, will be able to separate us from the love of God, which is in Christ Jesus our Lord."

22. Every Believer is **Sanctified**. (*1* Corinthians. *1:2)* "to the assembly of God which is at Corinth; those who are sanctified in Christ Jesus, called to be saints, with all who call on the name of our Lord Jesus Christ in every place, both theirs and ours:" (Sanctified means to be set apart. We are set apart from the world and in Christ Jesus.)

23. Every Believer is the **Temple of God**. (1 Corinthians *3:16)* "Don't you know that you are a temple of God, and that God's Spirit lives in you?" See also **1 Corinthians 6:19-20**.

24. Every Believer is **sealed with the Holy Spirit** of Promise. (*2* Corinthians. *1:22)"who also sealed us, and gave us the down payment of the Spirit in our hearts."* See also *Ephesians. 1:13-14*.

**25.** Every Believer is a **new Creation in Christ**. (*2* Corinthians *5:17*) *"Therefore if anyone is in Christ, he is a new creation. The old things have passed away. Behold, all things have become new."*

**26.** Every Believer is **Christ's' purchased possession.** (Ephesians 1:13-14) *"in whom you also, having heard the word of the truth, the Good News of your salvation—in whom, having also believed, you were sealed with the Holy Spirit of promise, who is a pledge of our inheritance, to the redemption of God's own possession, to the praise of his glory."*

**27.** Every Believer **is a Child of light**. ( *Ephesians 5:8*) *"For you were once darkness, but are now light in the Lord. Walk as children of light."*

**28.** Every Believer is **made complete in Him**.(*Colossians 2:10*) *"and in him you are made full, who is the head of all principality and power."*

**29.** Every Believer has **an eternal inheritance**. (*Hebrews 9:15*) *"For this reason he is the mediator of a new covenant, since a death has occurred for the redemption of the transgressions that were under the first covenant, that those who have been called may receive the promise of the eternal inheritance."*

**30.** Every Believer is a **gift from God to Christ**. (*John 17:6*) *"I revealed your name to the people whom you have given me out of the world. They were yours, and you have given them to me. They have kept your word." (Ephesians 1:18) "having the eyes of your hearts enlightened, that you may know what is the hope of his calling, and what are the riches of the glory of his inheritance in the saints."*

The following statements show some of the results of applying the above truths to your life:

A. When you recognize the value and worth God has placed on you, then you realize that you can have confidence in your relationship with God.

B. When you recognize who you are in your faith, then you realize that you are actually sinning by having a poor self image. Why should a child of God who shares in all the inheritance of Christ, whose home is heaven, and whose eternal friend is God, feel inferior about themselves?

C. When you recognize what God has done for you, then you realize that God is truly on your side.

D. When you realize all of what God has done for you to make you secure in your faith, you will no longer have to question and live in doubt about your eternity.

E. When you realize what God has done for you, then your faith will increase in value for you recognize that God has greatly invested in you.

F. When you realize what God has done for you, then you will not fear facing this God, because you go to him as a loved child.

Every Christmas you hear stories of children getting a truck load of toys and gifts and before very long they are tired of just about all of them. Few of these gifts gain great value to them. Before New Year's Day they are bored and don't know what to do.

This is not the case with the blessings God gives to each believer. The more we learn about them the more we see their intrinsic value. The further along we get in our walk with God the more we will appreciate these benefits. Become very familiar with these blessings that God has provided for you. Learn to draw on the benefit of these blessings as you face the difficult times in your life. Read over these often and learn to recognize just how these blessings will benefit your life.

# The Journey Begins

Normally this last section would be entitled "Conclusion". That's too predictable, and that is not the case if you decide to put the teaching of this book into practice. The Christian life is a journey. On a long journey you learn much about life. You learn how to handle yourself in difficult and different situations. You learn how to deal with people of different backgrounds. You learn to wait when there is no one to help you, or you are experiencing unexpected delays, because you don't know what to do.

In humility you recognize who you are and willingly accept your position in the body of Christ and the kind of service to which God calls you and you endure the learning process that it takes to make you more proficient in your walk and service. You step out by faith into the unknown realizing that God is there to help you. What bothered you when you first started your journey now no longer bothers you, and you take things in stride. What was difficult when you first tried something is now quite easy to do. What used to be a step into the darkness is now illuminated by faith in a friend, the experience of trusting God and the understanding from His word.

Your journey will last a life time. Be patient. Wait on God. Allow the Spirit of God to lead you. Be confident that God has your back and has your best interest in mind. When it seems like God has forgotten you, don't worry, He's still there. He just wants you to trust him and believe that He never changes his opinion about you as well as His commitment to you.

Come back to this book on occasion and read it or review it to see if there are areas that can help you in your maturing process. Experience helps you see life differently and gives you more understanding than you had at the beginning. You will be ready to take on some of these challenges with a new energy.

As you face different and difficult situations in life, you will find that the teachings of this book will help you or at least point you in the right direction. The more you know about your faith the greater will be your experiences and joy. As you travel life's road enjoy talking with Jesus and learning of Him. You have chosen the right path, so do not turn back; just enjoy the adventure.

Written and compiled by Rev. James Olah
Contact the author at: Jso46@hotmail.com

Study Guide

A study guide is provided in this book to help you go deeper in your personal study as well as in your family or small group discussion.

# Study guide for discipleship groups
## Using this study Guide

A. This study guide can be used in a small group, Sunday school class, or a discussion group.

B. This study guide can also be used in a family setting. The age of family members will regulate what questions you use or reword. They are good discussion starters for family talks. Family devotions should not be one person doing all the talking, but the leader should be a facilitator for discussion. Learn to discover each individual's thinking process on various topics. Get each one to think and welcome what they have to say.

C. When used with various ages, make sure you make the questions age appropriate. Many of the questions have several questions. Answer what you can. Some of the questions are difficult. This is done to make you think, search out, and ask other people to help you come to an understanding of the answer. If you find someone that can help you with these questions, they will also be there for you when you need them in other areas.

D. This study guide can be used in your personal growth time.

E. The other reason I offer several difficult questions is to make you stronger. Most study guides only have a few questions. Each number in this book usually has multiple questions to take you further into the topic. If you only lifted a five pound weight, you would not become much stronger. Just as a light weight would not build you up, easy questions will not cause you to think and dig deeper. If you lift one hundred pounds regularly, it will help you increase your strength to a good degree. In the same way difficult questions require you to think more critically and completely, search more diligently, and pray more passionately. Be willing to wrestle with a question for several days, maybe weeks before asking someone else. Search God's word and see what you can learn. The way you learn to dig now, even though it may be difficult, will prepare you to engage more readily in the future when problems of life need to be solved. There is nothing more satisfying than to reach a correct conclusion because of your diligence. Be willing to work hard to learn the truths of God that define your faith.

F. I do not apologize for making this portion a bit more difficult. There are too many books on Christian growth that are a lot of fluff. You feel good right away, but you take little away that really changes your life. Growth takes work and commitment. I encourage you to commit yourself to serious study.

# Chapter 1 - Become familiar with basic doctrines of the faith

1. Before looking back at the first chapter what are the five fundamental doctrines of the faith? Why do you think these five are so important?
2. Many people don't think that doctrine is important. They relegate the teaching of doctrine to church services that are dull and boring. They see little practical use for doctrine. Why do you think doctrine is so important to know? How can knowing the key doctrines affect the way you face life and live out your faith? Recall how knowing doctrine has affected some of your decisions. How can knowing doctrine affect the way you face trials in life? How can doctrine affect the way you act around your friends and peers at work? How can doctrine affect the way you act in your family?
3. Concerning the doctrine of the Bible (Bibliology) share why you think this one is so important. How does knowing this doctrine affect your life in a practical way? Learn more about the doctrine of the Bible at: http://bible.org/seriespage/survey-bible-doctrine-bible
4. Someone has said, "Without correct doctrine it is impossible to have correct conduct". How does knowing correct doctrine help you in living the Christian life?(2 Timothy 3:16-17)
5. The Bible contains doctrine for the purpose of establishing truth to help us understand God and His ways, as well as how we are to live by telling us how to relate to God and what is right and wrong in life. Read Romans 3 in class and together come up with as many references to doctrine as you can. Use the list of doctrines in chapter one or in your own church's doctrinal statement to remind you what the major ones are.
6. Some people have said: "Why don't we all forget doctrine and just get along?" Is that a good statement or not? Defend your answer. What would you say to that person?
7. Everyone wants to go to heaven and no one wants to go to hell. Many minimize the terribleness of hell or even deny its existence. Why do you think the doctrine of heaven and hell is important?
8. On your own: Read through the doctrinal statement and think of practical ways you can make that teaching relevant to your life. For instance: God is omnipresent, i.e. everywhere present. That means that God sees all you do, knows what you're facing in life, and is always there to help you. He knows what you are doing, even when you sin. How would keeping that in mind affect the rest of your day?

# Chapter 2 - SHARING YOUR FAITH

1. Every person has some fears when it comes to sharing the gospel with others. What are your most powerful fears that prevent you from sharing your faith with the lost? List 3-4.
2. There are people in your life who don't take the things of God seriously. If they died this week you just know they would not go to heaven. Does it concern you that they are not right to meet God? List three to five people in your life who are not saved.
3. How would you pray for these people? What needs to happen in their life for them to become more aware of their need and want to do something about it?
4. There are different ways to reach people. We all have different personalities and gifts that cause us to live and relate with people in different ways. God has equipped us to share the gospel in our unique way. Learn what your evangelism style is. Take the test at the following location and discover your style of evangelism: http://www.repentandturn.com/EvangelismStylesQuiz.html
5. At this website read up on the styles that the test indicates are your two strongest styles.
6. Who are people you know in church that fit into each of the evangelism styles?
7. Plan out a strategy, using your evangelism style, to reach one to two of your friends.
8. You are traveling by plane to a vacation destination, and you engage the person alongside of you in conversation. Along the way they find out you are a Christian, and they say they have been impressed by the Christian faith but would like you to explain how a person can know they can go to heaven. What basic truths of the gospel do you need to share with them so they can make an informed decision to trust Christ? Write out a sample prayer that you would encourage them to use to express their need and faith to God.

# Chapter 3 - FUTURE OF YOUR FAITH

1.  What benefit comes to your mind in knowing what the future holds for you as a Christian and for the world? How does knowing what God is going to do prevent you from living in fear?

2.  What is your reaction to *Revelation 14:9-12*? It reads *"Another angel, a third, followed them, saying with a great voice, "'If anyone worships the beast and his image, and receives a mark on his forehead, or on his hand, he also will drink of the wine of the wrath of God, which is prepared unmixed in the cup of his anger. He will be tormented with fire and sulfur in the presence of the holy angels, and in the presence of the Lamb. The smoke of their torment goes up forever and ever. They have no rest day and night, those who worship the beast and his image, and whoever receives the mark of his name. **Here** is the patience of the saints, those who keep the commandments of God, and the faith of Jesus.'"* Consider the word ***HERE*** in the last verse. It refers to what was said before it. How do you think God wants such a thought to affect you?

3.  God is very open in making known the things He is going to do in this world. Why does God tell us what will happen in the future? How does knowing the future affect the way you live in this world? How should it define your purpose?

4.  The author of this book holds to a Pre-tribulation Rapture as presented in this chapter. Do you agree with his reasons for holding to such a position? If not, what view do you hold and why? If so, why do you agree?

5.  What are the coming judgments on humanity? In which one will you be judged? Some of the details of the coming judgments are found in: Matthew 25:31-46; 1 Corinthians 3:11-14; Revelation 20:4-6 and 20:11-15; 2 Corinthians 5:8-10. The last judgment in this list is the one where Christians will be judged. Which crown are you pursuing in your Christian life? Do you think a Christian can win more than one?

6.  1 Thessalonians 4:13-18 talks about the rapture of the church. Use your imagination and describe what that may look like to the world when all the believers are suddenly gone. What kind of devastation might be on this earth? If you want to read a fiction series that puts the events of Revelation into story form read the Left Behind series by Tim LaHaye and Jerry Jenkins. http://www.leftbehind.com/

7.  Do you think it is important to talk with non-believers about what the Bible says is going to happen in this world? If not, why? If so, why? How can talking about prophecy be a door to sharing the gospel?

8.  How should the imminent return of Christ affect the way that Christians plan and conduct their lives? If you knew that Jesus was going to return in thirty days, how would you act differently? How would that time table affect your boldness in talking with the lost? What would be most important to you?

# Chapter 4 - GROWTH IN YOUR FAITH

1. Why do you think so many people who become Christians don't take spiritual grow seriously? Do you think that the person who never grows in their faith is a genuine believer? Why? See Matthew 7:15-23

2. As you consider each of the main points in this section, which two of these seem most important for you to develop as a Christian? Why do you give them top priority?

3. One of the benefits of being a Christian is that we have a direct line to the living God. Just think of it; the creator of the universe knows you and will listen to your requests. He wants to help you; to help you pray properly He has given instruction spread throughout the Bible. Since you have been saved, what has impressed you about the privilege of prayer?

4. You would think that Christians would want to learn how to live the new life. It would seem that being obedient to the teaching in the Bible and the leading of the Holy Spirit would be important. Yet many Christians find that to be unimportant, and they exempt themselves from obedience. Name four reasons that Christians do not obey God. Can you find a verse that calls us to obey God's word? Give four benefits of obeying God's word.

5. When we consider the importance of fellowship with God we need to learn how to maintain such fellowship. One of the things that hinders our fellowship with God (1 John 1:5-9) is our sin. How can a God who is light (absolute purity) have fellowship with a willfully sinful child? 1 John 1:9 tells us that the way we deal with our known sin is to confess our sin. What does it means to confess sin? How do you respond when you confess your sin and you don't feel forgiven? How does faith fit in with your feelings when you don't feel forgiven? What is the significance of God being just in forgiving your sin? What do you think the verse is referring to after it says "to forgive us for our sin" and then goes on to say "and to cleanse us from all unrighteousness"? If our sins are forgiven, why do we need to be cleansed from all unrighteousness?

6. God equips us to have a significant part in the body of Christ. He does this by giving us a spiritual gift. Before you come to class take the online spiritual gift inventory and find out what spiritual gift you have. You might want to go on line and find a couple of others and take them too. They all differ in various ways and this will help you be more familiar with the gifts. Take the time to read the definition of your strongest gifting. Tell others in the group what your gift is. Then talk about how you can use that gift in your church. Do others see that in you? Why is using one's gift linked to spiritual growth?

7. There are many Christians who have not grown in their faith. In life there are illustrations of people and things that do not come to maturity. For instance, when you see a person who is mentally challenged or handicapped, you realize that they will never be able to reach their full potential. Share with the group illustrations of things that disappoint you in life when they don't come to maturity. How is that a picture of the Christian who does not mature in their faith?

8. Concluding on a positive note, who is a mature Christian that impresses you? What strikes you about the way they conduct their life? What examples in their lives inspire you? Which qualities in their lives impress you enough that you would like to develop in your own life?

# Chapter 5 - DEFENSE OF YOUR FAITH

1. If a person cannot defend their faith, what negative effects can that have on their progress or growth? What often happens to young people who go to college and don't know how to defend their faith?
2. Atheists often claim that Christians have a blind faith when it comes to God and believing the Bible. Describe how atheists actually have a blind faith in what they believe about evolution and the afterlife.
3. If someone were to ask you how you defend your belief that the Bible is the Word of God, how would you respond? Why is this truth such an important point to know how to defend?
4. It is important to have a mindset that we have to defend our faith. Skeptics will look for every means possible to disprove the Bible and the existence of God. When they can't disprove something, they will call you names or minimize your reasoning ability. In that way they don't have to deal with the truth. Why is this so important to them? What do you think is their motivation in being tenacious in their effort?
5. We are in more than a battle of intellects. We are in a spiritual battle. When we got saved we traded sides. We were children of darkness, i.e. the devil, and now we are children of light, i.e. God. We are warned that we have an enemy in the spirit world who is seeking to destroy us and our effectiveness for God. (Ephesians 6:10-17, 1 Peter 5:8-9) How does the Ephesians passage add to our understanding of the battle in which we are engaged? In the Peter passage what are we told to do that actually includes apologetics? How do we resist Satan? Do you think the atheist serves him or God?
6. When you gain a working knowledge of why you believe what you do and are able to understand the issues, how does such knowledge make you stronger? First, when you understand the reasons why you believe what you do, you are now able to counter the attacks of skeptics. Secondly, you are also able to help other Christians become stronger in their faith. How might Satan react to a Christian who is strong in their faith in this way? Why is it important to know that you may come under such attack?
7. Apologetics is not just a defense of the beliefs that are presented in the Bible, but it is also an analytical look at other religions to see how they compare to the teachings of the Bible. We talked about skeptics who attack the Bible in previous questions. The issue here is that there are false teachers, and we must know how to evaluate them and stand for the truth. The key in talking with cults and other religions is to understand their terminology. They often say the same thing we do, but they attach totally different meanings to fit their theology. Why is it important to be able to

detect the error in other religions? How does knowing what another religion believes before you talk with them assist you in helping them?

8. There are many ways our faith is attacked. We hear people say there is no such thing as absolute truth. Such a statement is an oxymoron in itself. Others will say what truth is for you does not apply to them. They tell you that you can't establish a standard set of morals for everyone. You can't speak against people who believe differently than you. You see this in the battle that is ensuing in the issue of homosexuality, marriage and abortion. How do you prepare to defend your position and then engage such issues in our society today? Does being called a name prevent you from engaging in these important issues?

# Chapter 6 - DETERMINING THE QUESTIONABLE AREAS OF LIFE

1.  God does not tell us everything we should and should not do. The Bible gives us principles to determine these undefined areas. What are some of the questionable or undefined areas that you have noticed in the Christian life?

2.  Do you think everyone will come to the same conclusions as to what is right or wrong in their undefined areas of life? Read Romans 14 and you will see that what might be right for one Christian might be equally wrong for another. Remember we are talking about undefined areas of life not the clearly defined areas as spelled out in Scripture. Some Christians might think it is all right to drink alcohol in moderation and others think it is intolerable. Some might go to movies and others not. In Paul's time one of the questions was whether a Christian should eat meat offered to idols. Who does Paul say is the weaker brother in this debate?

3.  Do you think it is imperative that we avoid doing something that we might think is unacceptable before God, but a weaker believer does not think it wrong? If we refrain ourselves, are we obligated to refrain from doing it when they are not around? Does their weakness now regulate our lives?

4.  The reading section gives a list of biblical principles to help regulate our decisions. Can you think of any other scriptural principles that should regulate our decision making process? Why do you think it is important that we use scriptural principles rather than good old fashioned logic?

5.  If you think of allowing the weaker Christian's views to regulate your life, when does their request or demands become legalistic? Legalism is when people go beyond scripture and set up standards by which everyone else is to live in order to please God or do right. Paul gave into the legalism sometimes to gain the opportunity to be a witness to the Jews. Other times he blasted it and called it for what it was. So the question is this: When does the weakness of the immature brother go beyond a reasonable request to a legalistic claim on your life? (This is not an easy question. Even if you don't come to a good conclusion, I want you to be aware of the issue and learn to take the stand that God's Spirit leads you to take. Take some time to grapple with it before you write it off.)

6.  If you have had to use principles taught in the chapter to make a decision in an undefined area, share with the group some of your struggles and how you came to your conclusion.

7.  (Just read and discuss) Sometimes arguments over the undefined areas of life have caused divisions in the church. Make sure that you allow people to have different opinions in these areas. Treat them with respect. Don't blow it out of proportion. Be kind. Remember they are your brothers or

sisters in Christ. Sometimes when people blow things out of proportion, and people take sides the church has a division and some people leave. If things get ugly enough the church splits and a lot of people leave. The only winner in such a situation is not the work of God, but the side of Satan. He loves to see God's people fight and feud over insignificant things. Don't let Satan get the best of you or your church. Have you seen this happen on some scale? Did people respond in an honorable way? How should they have responded in a realistic way that honored scripture?

8.  God has not defined openly all that is right but has instead given us principles that he wants us to think through and reason out under the influence of the Holy Spirit. It may not really matter to God if you take one side of the issue or the other. He wants you to love people who have different opinions and views than you. How do you think the teaching of the following passage should affect the way you respond to those who aren't taking the same view you are in the undefined issues? (John 11:34-35) "A new commandment I give to you, that you love one another, just like I have loved you; that you also love one another. By this everyone will know that you are my disciples, if you have love for one another."

# Chapter 7 - CREATOR IN OUR FAITH

1. Why do you think God wants us to know He is our creator? What kind of negative effect does not believing in the creator have on society?

2. Knowing that God is the creator has far-reaching affects on our life as well as on society. How does recognizing God as creator affect our outlook on life? How does it affect our view of our self and who we are? How does it affect the way we look at others and the way we treat them? How does it affect our view on the unborn? How does it affect the way we think of the purpose of our life?

3. When we recognize that God is our creator, we then acknowledge that He knows every aspect of our life, He knows how we best function, and He has a specific purpose for our life. Why would anyone put so much thought into the design of something and then not have a purpose for it? Why would one make something and not know how it properly functions? How should such knowledge affect the confidence you have in the way God guides you? How should such knowledge affect the way you pray to God? How should such knowledge affect your view on the Ten Commandments and the moral teaching from God in the Bible?

4. Part of our prayer life is to show appreciation for God and what he has done. How can being out in nature and noticing the diverse details of nature affect the way you worship? How can knowing the intricacies of the human body cause you to praise and worship God? If God is the creator, then His creation should declare His glory, ability, and creativity. The more we know about God's creation the more we know the mind of God and are better able to worship Him with understanding and appreciation. That is the kind of freshness that God desires in our worship of Him.

5. Recognize that God is the creator who made the world out of nothing, and brought it all into being by the command of his voice. The next time you are outside and alone shout out for something to come into existence. What happens? How much power do you have to bring something into being with your voice? God spoke and brought the birds, the fish, and the animals into being. God took the clay of the ground and made man. Can we ask anything too big for our God? Why are you afraid to ask God to do great things that would accomplish His will on earth? We pray to Creator God when we pray, and there is nothing too hard for Him.

6. Read through the two sections in chapter seven: "If Creation is True What Would You Expect to See in Research?" "If Evolution is True What Would You Expect to See in Research?" How might this section help you in talking about evolution and creation? What might you add to this list

that would help people to better evaluate the issues? What do you see as important issues in the creation / evolution debate?

7. Often the evolutionists seek to debunk creationism by saying that it is faith-based rather than science-based. If man was not there in the beginning and cannot test what happened by true science then how does he draw an opinion? His answer does not come through science but like anyone else, who doesn't know an answer, he guesses. There is another way to learn about what happened when no man was around to see. We should seek an answer from someone who was there and saw it happen. God was there and He revealed that He is the creator. The very first words in the Bible declare this fact. He wanted us to know that He was there and He brought the world and life into being. Should not the one who gave us the ability to think and reason also be able to communicate with us? Many say that because we can't explain how God began, we have the same problem that the evolutionists have about the beginning of matter. We really don't have to explain how God began. He has not revealed it to us, other than saying that He is from all eternity. The fact of the matter is that God revealed He was the first cause of matter, and He was the creator of all things. Revelation from an eyewitness about the unknown trumps guesses any day in my book. When it comes to how matter started you would have to say that evolutionary science is really a blind faith kind of "science". Why do you think that scientists are so adamantly opposed to the logic of there being a designer / creator of this world? How does revelation about the unknown oppose evolutionary philosophy?

8. When you notice the great beauty of creation around you and the intricate design of the plants, fish and animals, you recognize that God is into detail, beauty and functionality. How does that affect the way you interpret Revelation 21:1-2? What is the significance of saying that the New Jerusalem is like a bride beautifully dressed for her husband?

# Chapter 8 - SINS AGAINST YOUR FAITH

1. People don't like you telling them what is right or wrong. It used to be that people knew what sin was. They may not have been living in a way to please God, but they knew it was a sin to commit adultery, be involved in homosexuality, be drunk, take drugs, steal, lie, or kill (and the biblical list of sins goes on). What advantage is it to know what things are right or wrong in life?

2. Our society has experienced great changes morally. In this post-Christian era, fewer people recognize the authority of God and His moral standards. Just because man's views have changed, doesn't mean that God's views have changed. What kinds of things are not called sin today that we recognized as sin in years gone by?

3. What part do you think television, media, music and the secularization of schools has played in changing the moral values of society?

4. The Bible lists sins, but often does not tell why they are so bad. Choose a couple of the sins and talk about the fallout of being involved in them. From experiences of life what kinds of consequences have you seen as a result of people being involved in specific sins? One sin will often lead to another. For example, when a person commits adultery they will lie to their spouse and others.

5. Why do you think God puts limits on us in the moral areas? What is he declaring by establishing standards in such areas as adultery, stealing, killing and lying?

   Every sin that you indulge in wins your affection and devotion by a lie. Recognizing the lies that seduced you into sin is the first step in breaking free. When you find yourself doing something wrong, ask yourself "What is the lie I believed to justify doing this?" Here is an example: Why did I start drinking? Was it to be popular and accepted by my peers? Was it to feel good so I could party? Did it help me forget? Did it accomplish what I wanted it to? Perhaps reality questions might include: Did it actually affect me more than I expected? Did it take away my money? Did it make me feel miserable? Did it take away my inhabitations so that I did some really stupid things? Did I lose some friends because of it? Did I get into trouble while drunk? Did I like the feeling of puking in the toilet? Did I enjoy the hangover the next day? What lies drew me into my sin? What lies did I overlook once I got into it? There are some sins you have gotten involved in earlier in your life. What kind of lies drew you into your sins? Share some of the less embarrassing ones with the group. *On your own* consider examining the lies that are keeping you in sin today. Sin is never a benefit to you and in order to break its hold you must understand the lie that is keeping you enslaved to that sin, and replace it with truth.

6. How do you look at your personal sin? Do you minimize how bad it is, or do you recognize its harm to your life, as well as its harm to your relationship with God? We minimize our sin by failing to recognize the seriousness of what we are doing, and the harm it brings into life. It seems like when we do something it isn't as bad as when someone else does it to us. One of the ways we turn attention away from our sin is to accuse others of sins. The more we can put others down, the less likely we are to be accused by them of our sins and failures. Why is it so hard to admit our sin? The church would be much different if people openly dealt with personal sin quickly instead of looking to accuse others?

7. Romans 6:23 states that "The wages of sin is death." Paul is speaking to Christians in this passage. As you read this chapter you find that God expects us to no longer be slaves to sin. The passage does not say that the believer loses his/her salvation because of sin, but says you earn death by your sin. What do you think Paul means by that statement that the wages of sin is death?

8. What sins do we tend to think are socially acceptable even in the Church? Why do you think we minimize the seriousness of gossip, sinful pride, profanity, watching porn, reading romance novels that paint a false view of relationships or other such sins?

# Chapter 9 - Worldview and how it affects you

1. Before you read this chapter, how much did you know about worldview? After you read this chapter did your perception change? What aspect of worldview do you think is most important?

2. One of the reasons we need to understand worldview is because our country is so diversified in its ethnicity, beliefs and values. We need to be able to make distinction between right and wrong in society. What do you see happening among believers because they don't recognize how worldviews affect the direction of their life? What do you think our society would look like if Christians were living out their worldview because they believed it to be true?

3. What kind of world view do you think Hollywood is pushing on society? Name specifics. What about your local public school?

4. Why do you think it is important for a couple getting married to have the same worldview? Why do you think so few Christians don't think that having a compatible worldview is important?

5. What are some ways that we can teach children and young people to distinguish the differences in worldviews?

6. How do you think young people will engage their beliefs when they have a proper worldview? Think of this question in light of what they face at school from teachers and from their friends. Tolerance is promoted oft times as nothing more than a method of shutting people up who have a point or opinion that differs from their own. Also, there are moral issues relating to abortion, homosexuality, and sex outside of marriage as being acceptable. Schools usually focus on being safe rather than promoting the benefits of abstinence and morality. The more knowledgeable you get about worldview the more intentional you can be in looking for ways to apply worldview to every aspect of your life.

7. Come to class with the "personal study project" completed, as presented in chapter nine. It said: Using the first 12 chapters of Genesis, record the worldview God wants you to learn in order to regulate life. (Example: God is creator; God made both men and women to be like they are; marriage is established by God, God's instruction about eating meat, etc.) Developing your worldview based on God's word makes it more personal. Share with the class what really struck you as important to God as you formulated your biblical worldview.

8. Have you listened to something on television, and what they said just didn't sound right, nor did it have a ring of truth to it? Learn to notice the use of a person's worldview as you watch National Geographic, or History Channel or the Learning Channel. Usually when they talk about the Bible, they pick "experts" that don't respect or acknowledge the

Christian worldview. The perspectives of the people they interview usually have a liberal slant to their evaluation. Often they don't believe in the authority of God's word, miracles, the resurrection or the historical accuracy of the Bible. The next time you watch one of the programs that focuses on some aspect of Christianity, listen with a more critical mindset. Then do your own research on the internet with conservative scholars and see what they have to say about the same thing. Remember all the scholars in the world mean nothing if they are not basing their observations and conclusions on truth. Have you picked up on any of this liberal mindset on programs you have watched? Share that with the group.

# Chapter 10 – A Self-examined Life

1.  Socrates said: "The unexamined life is not worth living for a human being." Have you ever checked the oil in your car only to find out it doesn't registered on the dip stick? What would have happened if you continued to drive the car without examining the oil? It could have led to the ruin of your car. This section offers you the opportunity to examine your Christian life. It reminds you that it needs personal examination. Most churches have communion at least once a month in order to afford you opportunity to examine your life. What kind of benefit do you think such an examination can do to your life? Also notice this same command in Galatians 6:4: "But let each man test his own work, and then he will take pride in himself and not in his neighbor."

2.  *Project for group.* Take one of the following passages and write out, individually or as a group ten self-examination questions based on the content. (Ephesians 4:22-32; Philippians 3:7-17; Colossians 12-25; James 4:1-12; 2 Peter 1:1-11 & 3:18; 1 John 4:7-21)

3.  Sometimes we are afraid of truth. We think that if we admit our weaknesses we are failures. The opposite is actually true. How many times have you listened to a person tell about their addiction or moral failure and then talk about how he recognized his wrong and God helped him to change? Don't you think he had fears in sharing that with you? Why do you think others would have less respect for you if you admitted your failure? Admitting our failures is the door to growth and vibrancy in our faith. Our church has a college group that has leaders who are very transparent. One night the speaker shared the struggles he had at a certain point in his life. The result was that when we broke into small groups the rest was more open to sharing about their struggles. What prevents you from admitting your failure and choosing to work on change?

4.  It is when we have to face our fears alone that we feel most helpless. Take a few minutes and write out a prayer in which you acknowledge your fears and request help from God's Spirit to empower you, to give you wisdom, and to help you. Reading your prayer to the group is optional. Don't feel bad if you don't feel comfortable sharing it publicly. Just tell the group you pass. For those of you that do share, realize that this not only helps you formulate your thoughts, but it can also encourage others in their quest of self examination. Writing out your prayer to God is also a way of acknowledging your fears without having to tell everyone else.

5.  If you don't have this checklist when you come to communion time, choose four areas that you will examine in your life each time. Here is a suggested list. You can choose or develop four that are more fitting to your life:

a. Have I been indulging in sinful thoughts?
b. Have I been treating people in my family in a Christian way?
c. Have I been taking my faith seriously by reading God's word regularly, applying God's word to my life and obeying God?
d. What actions in my life do I need to address more seriously?

What kind of questions would you make as part of your list? Write out your questions in the back of your Bible or print them off on a book mark that you can have available the next time you have communion and need to examine your life.

6. We have talked about you examining your life during communion, but this kind of action ought to be done fairly regularly in your life. The more you do it and respond to it, the more it will change your life and move you on to greater maturity. This is important early on in your faith. If you have a close friend, consider doing something like this with them. How could self examination work with a person you consider a mentor? How might that look in a real-life situation?

7. When you go to the doctor he has a set of check-up procedures. Get weighed. Take blood pressure. Listen to heart. Take pulse. Anyone who goes to a doctor knows the routine. If you were asked to develop three daily self-examination questions to help you keep on track spiritually, what would they be?

8. What do most people do during communion when we are told to examine our lives? What do you do during that time? What do you think about? Do you do something that actually affects your spiritual condition? Do you address how you can act or respond differently to people when you get out of Church? Are you making plans for the coming week without thought of change? Do you just want the service to get over? This chapter provides a good list of questions you can use during communion to make it spiritually meaningful. During closing prayer, in group take about five minutes for each person to be by themselves with the questions they wrote out in question two (or choose a section from the book).

# Chapter 11 – Forgiving as a Christian

1. People do terrible things in this world. Perhaps you are the victim of something terrible because of a person's thoughtlessness, carelessness or just because they were outright mean. What kind of purpose do you think God wants you to learn when he tells you to forgive that person?

2. There are many people we forgive during a lifetime. Some are easy to forgive, and there are some who wrong us that we just find it hard, and maybe feel it is impossible to forgive. What kind of motivation should help us to obey God in this area? If you have worked through something like this, share it with the rest of the group. Share your struggles and the benefits you experienced by forgiving.

3. Sometimes when we forgive, we have preconceived ideas of how the other person should respond. We think they should be grateful, but usually they don't acknowledge it. We can't let their wrong response prevent us from forgiving them or others. Our motivation is to obey Christ. Another preconceived idea that we have is that if we forgive someone our relationship is supposed to be immediately reconciled and then we must be ready to carry on from where it left off. Sometimes that is true. Does forgiveness always mean reconciliation? Why or why not? Do some offenses call for something to be done to effect reconciliation? Examples: Mate commits adultery. Someone steals from you. Someone destroyed a power tool that you loaned them. A person lies to you.

4. How should you handle your responsibility to forgive if you don't feel like forgiving that person? Does forgiving them mean that you tell them that you forgive them, or is it enough to just forgive them before God with a statement like "I forgive Jason for turning his back on me in that terrible situation."

5. When you forgive a person will it make you feel like everything is settled right away? Do you think sometimes forgiveness is a process in which you may have to forgive the person a hundred times the first day or two, and then it dwindles down over the next few weeks or months? Has your experience shown you that you have to forgive them again maybe years later when you start to think about your hurt again?

6. When I have preached on forgiveness, I have discovered that more people respond because that is an area in which they have not been handling properly and want to know how to do it. They also have of questions about how to approach their offender. Do you find it hard to forgive someone in your life? Why do you think that is so? What advice would you give to someone who was having difficulty in forgiving a person who really hurt them?

7. Which of the verses given in this section stand out to you as the most important? Give your reason why you selected this verse(s).

8. What do we do if we have offended someone and need to ask forgiveness? Is it all right to think that they will forget it? Most people don't. How do you think you should approach a person you have wronged in order to ask their forgiveness? Is it sufficient to say, "I'm sorry that happened?" "I'm sorry that you were offended." "I was wrong, but so where you." What could be wrong with those statements? How might you request forgiveness in which you acknowledge the wrong you did? Write a list of what forgiveness is. Also write a list of what forgiveness is not.

# Chapter 12 - Bible Study: Food for Growth

1. Why is food so important to life? How is Bible study like your food?

2. What do you think is so significant about Jesus' response to Satan when he says "It is written, 'Man shall not live by bread alone, but by every word that proceeds out of the mouth of God'"? (Matthew 4:4) What does that declare about the importance of the Word of God to you?

3. The Word of God is essential to spiritual growth. It gives us understanding about God and His ways, it helps us understand the issues of life, it informs us about the future, it enlightens us to what God did to provide redemption as well as how to be saved. Why do so many Christians neglect reading and studying the Bible? If the Bible is the Word of God that is food to our spiritual life, how do you think that neglect affects the dynamics of one's spirituality? Do you think a Christian who does not take a personal interest in Bible study can grow as close to God as one who does? How can Bible study help draw one closer to God? What advice would you give to a person who was not reading their Bible? Would your advice come from one who experiences the fulfillment of reading the Bible on your own, or would it come as one who knows the right words? (These questions are not meant to be trivial but to get you thinking about your personal involvement.)

4. Have you developed a Bible reading/study schedule for yourself? If so share with the class what you do. If not then there are some things to keep in mind. Where will you read? How often? What time? Will you use a devotional book or read through the Bible? If you are new, start in the New Testament and read it through. You don't have to read it in order.

5. One of the assignments of developing your Bible study skills is to choose a verse to memorize. Find Psalm 119:11 and go around the room and have each one read it from their Bible. By the time you do this most of you should have it memorized. Now go around the room and each one quote the verse without looking at it. (Now, that didn't hurt did it?) "I have hidden your word in my heart that I might not sin against you." (Psalm 119:11)

6. Tell about the most interesting thing you have learned as you read or studied your Bible.

7. Share with the group how regular reading of the Bible has helped you.

8. Read Deuteronomy 32:46-47b and discuss the importance that Moses places on the word of God in the life of a believer. What are the significant phrases in this passage? What do you think of Moses' statement when he says "it is your life"?

# Chapter 13 - Never forget who you are

1. Name three of the blessings God has provided you, at the moment of salvation that really gets your motor revving. If you wish, you may share why they impress you.

2. When you realize that God has done all of this for every believer, no matter how mature or immature they are, no matter how worthy or unworthy they are living, how does that regulate the way you should talk to or about another believer? When you ridicule and cut down another believer you are offending someone, whom Christ has redeemed, someone in whom the Holy Spirit lives, someone with whom you will spend eternity in heaven, someone that God loves so much that He was willing to send His Son to die on the cross. How does such truth affect the way you look at other believers?

3. When we find a good deal we like to tell people about it. We want them to benefit from the deal as well. We like to share good things. How much does the rich blessing of God excite you and affect your desire to go out and tell others where to find this great benefit? Do you think if more Christians were impressed with their salvation they would be more open in sharing their faith? How much of our refusal to share the gospel with the lost is motivated by our lack of being fully impressed with our salvation? (Be honest in your response. Don't lie to yourself.)

4. Why do you think God lavishes so much on each believer in their salvation? What kind of motivation would cause Him to go above and beyond? Why do you think He wants to impress and honor us when we don't deserve it?

5. The section ends with four statements about the importance of knowing this teaching. What effect should this teaching have on the way you view yourself, your worth and your significance? How should this affect the person who has poor self image or poor self worth? How should this affect the person who is being continually belittled and run down by someone that should love them? How should this affect the person who has been brutalized, raped or abused when they think of their worth? Men who traffic in young girls for prostitution will prepare them for their work by abusing them, raping them, hitting them and calling them names. When they are completely humiliated the girls feel like they are not important and don't try to resist any more. We have all been brutalized like that by Satan, and so we need the truth of what God has done for us in learning to not just become what he wants us to be, but in recognizing our true worth before God, so we don't have to go through life feeling unimportant or insignificant.

6. Some parents will call their children dummies, and tell them they can't do anything right. They raise their children in a very negative environment. Good parents will raise their children in a positive environment. God wants to show Himself as a very positive parent in what He has done for us. How do you now translate that into the way you live your life? How do you allow the good things of your life to give you confidence to do great things for Him? Which of these truths might you share with other believers to give them greater confidence in their relationship with God or courage to take on greater things in life?

7. What kind of courage does it give you to take on the difficulties of life when you realize that "God is for us"? Why do you fear doing what the Spirit prompts you to do? Why do you think God will now let you down when He asks you to do what you think is impossible?

8. How can knowing all these things that God has done for you affect the way you treat the lost, your family, those who offend you, those at work/school, or those at church? How can Christians be more positive toward others?

## To the facilitator of the small group:

I have a couple years of experience with small groups. I was the Life Group Director in our church and I was in charge of training and writing monthly training newsletters. I've talked with group leaders and helped them work through their problems. I've written lesson material, teaching ideas, and strategies. As I think about using this material, I offer the following suggestions to help you in using this book. I trust that those in your group will benefit from the book and the discussion of it.

A. You don't have to answer every question. Pick the ones that best fit your people.

B. Don't embarrass people by calling on them if you don't know if they are comfortable in answering questions. Let them volunteer to answer on their own. You can also ask them privately if they are comfortable in answering questions.

C. If possible have people sit in a circle.

D. Small group is about building relationships, so celebrate holidays and birthdays. Plan fun events along the way. Use summer as an outreach time. Have cookouts, mini golfing, go watch fireworks, etc and invite people who are not in the group. Give outsiders time to get to know the group.

E. Establish ground rules for your group. No one is to laugh or make fun of someone for their answer, unless there is a joker who is fishing for a laugh. That which is personal in nature is not to leave that group. Under no circumstance is sensitive information learned about a person in the group to be shared with those outside the group. If what a person reveals indicates they are in danger or they will put someone in danger (suicide, etc), you need to inform them that you must go to proper authorities. When a person is talking no one else is to interrupt them or be carrying on conversation. That is just a courtesy. Ask that people be honest in their response. Last, but not least, start on time and end on time. If people want to stay after the end, that is okay. People need to be able to count on going home at a designated time. You don't know their schedule. Some people may like to talk a lot, but there might be one or two that don't like the drawn out meeting and may make that an excuse not to return.

F.  Because this is a discipleship program, get as many people involved as possible. Assign one of the people with leadership skills (a week ahead of time), to handle 2-4 of the questions. You do the rest, or ask someone else to do it. Look for people who feel comfortable in fielding questions. Asking the week ahead gives people time to review the questions and come up with their own answers so they can better facilitate conversation.

G.  When you ask a question, don't be afraid of "dead air." Allow people time to ruminate on the question. Make sure the question you are asking is clear. Wait until someone speaks; try not to be the one to break the silence because you are uncomfortable, unless the time is really long.

H.  Some of the questions are really pointed. Don't be afraid of delving into the tough questions.

I.  I am not giving you answers to the questions in the study guide. That means you need to think them out on your own before class.

J.  You know your group. If these questions don't meet the need of your group on a particular meeting night, make up your own questions that you think are relevant to them and related to the subject. Remember that study questions in any course are your servants, not your master. Questions are there to help facilitate discussion that is relevant to the topic. You may think that all or most of the questions have no relevance to your group. That shows you are thinking and know your people. But it will take work on your part to come up with your own questions or revise the ones provided for you.

K.  Get people to open up as much as possible. Don't do the majority of the talking. If you do all the talking, you don't know what they are thinking. Draw them out. Get others to respond to what they say. Guide the discussion, but don't dominate the discussion.

L.  There are some questions that require internet research. Let them know the week ahead of time to do that particular question. Computer research is relevant for the topic of styles of evangelism, spiritual gifts and worship styles. If you ask them to do any homework, give them only one task.

M.  This is a discipleship course, so one of the things you want to do is get people involved as much as possible. Have a regular prayer time in your group. Pray in groups of two or three. Use sentence prayer focused on a topic. For example: express to God one thing for which you are thankful, praise God for one of the great aspects of who He is, or pray for one or two people who have problems or illnesses. Have each one ask someone to pray for one of their unsaved friends. This kind of prayer will keep prayer times fresh. Find out each week how the people they prayed about last week are doing.

N. Food is an important part of small groups. Have light snacks. Encourage 1-2 people to supply snacks each week. Have a signup sheet so people can sign up. The host should provide beverages and utensils.

O. Have pencil and paper for those who may want to talk notes.

# Other Kindle Books by James Olah

## The Town of Salvation
*Book one of the "**Basic Christianity**" series*

Have you ever wondered why there are so many religions in the world? All religions claim they are the true one. Atheists also say that about their form of belief, and thus many belittle those who chose a faith different from theirs. If you were to evaluate the religions of the world, what criteria would you use to judge them to determine which one is right? It is imperative that you get that right, for your eternity depends on it. Since God devised salvation for errant man, it makes sense that he does not hide its truth from us.

If religion is really of God rather than just an expression of man's fears of how to explain the unexplainable or unknown in life, then you must look at the book that claims to be each religion's source of authority. Which one has a truly heavenly "tone" to it? Which one stands out as being different yet down to earth? If God is the creator of mankind and gave us our abilities, then certainly He knows how to effectively communicate truth with us.

This book starts with one of the reasons many religions have started. Man looks for a way to deal with his fear, the need of forgiveness, acceptance by God and a purpose that goes beyond this life.

I am biased as I write this book. We all write and communicate with our bias in life. My bias is toward the Christian faith. When I look at the religions of the world, I find them lacking when it comes to making a person right with God and preparing a person for heaven. Most of the religions of the world are a rehash of the same old thing. Christianity is absolutely unique in its holy book we call the Bible, in the view of man, in the means of salvation and the relationship it offers to mankind with God, and the way it changes people for the better. To show this difference I take you to a town called Salvation and show you in a unique manner the beliefs of some of the major religions of the world, and then spend time looking at the means of salvation talked about in the Bible. You make your own decision, but make sure you choose wisely.

I close the book with a detailed account of the biblical view of salvation, to help you understand it so you can make a decision to follow Christ, if that is your choice. This is done in the unique setting of going into God's Gift Shoppe and making the right "faith purchases".

**Town of Salvation** is a unique book in the explanation of salvation. Oft times you see a short pamphlet that invites one to become a Christian. The problem is that they don't often address the needs and concerns people have, nor do they go into the kind of detail it takes to make an informed decision. This book does that.

The gospel is short, but there are those who like to understand the details of why each component is important, and that is what I seek to do here.

This is also a good book to help the Christian better understand their own salvation, as well as to help those who want to join with God in the journey of life. This is the first of two books in the series on basic Christianity.

ASIN: B007ZJYA5A- **Kindle Books**
http://www.amazon.com/dp/B007ZJYA5A

**What is the Tone of Your Communication?**
*How tone changes your message or enhances your words*
*Guidelines for dealing with communication problems in relationships*

This book addresses how tone of voice affects the way you communicate. Many sabotage their relationship, not because of the words they speak but the way they speak their words. You can have the best intentions and love the other person dearly, but the way your words come out can kill their spirit or get them frustrated and angry. They may be ready to defend themselves from what they perceive is an attack, or fight to protect their honor. This eye-opening book will help you to not just see yourself but hear yourself better when you are talking with your loved one. Insightful questions and practical suggestions are offered in a thoughtful way to help you work through the problem areas. If you don't think you need this book, read it so you understand those around you who do have a problem with the way they use their tone of voice.

**Kindle Books: ASIN B004Y020KU – Also in print form**

**The Dynamics of Communication and Sex**
*Effective Keys to Preventing Relationship Breakdowns -*
*Enjoying the Benefits of Maintaining a Healthy Sex Life in your Marriage*

Every couple faces battles in their relationship which stem from them not understanding the greatest need and motivation of the other. We often think a person ought to just understand us or "get it" after a while. But when they don't, we think they are out to get us, don't truly care about us or worse yet, they seek to purposely offend us. That is where disappointment starts, the hurts begin, the battle line is drawn, and eventually the disagreements start. Fights don't usually happen instantly, but are often born out of a slow burn until unpleasant words become frequent. If you are passive / aggressive, it will be more of a quiet struggle, but the hurt feelings are just as real, for they are now underground rather than out in the open to properly address.

When a child is whiney at the end of a long day at Disney, you know it is because they are tired and have expended their energy. They are on overload and don't know how to handle it. You can't reason your child out of their irritable state. They just need sleep. You are patient with them because you understand their needs. We are willing to be patient with our children, but why are we so unwilling to respond to the needs of our spouse with the same kind of patient understanding? The purpose of this book is to help you appreciate the motivation of your mate. When you understand their motivation you can be more patient with them and seek to work with them more effectively.

Why does she have to talk and give every detail of what went on in the day? Why does he come home and reveal nothing or very little of what went on in his day but instead just wants to sit around and do nothing, or go out and play sports, or work in the garage? Do you know what motivates a woman to ask all those questions? Do you know her deepest need? Do you know of the loneliness in her soul? Do you know why a man doesn't think it is so important to connect with you by sharing the details of his day?

Why does he seem to have only one thing on his mind? How can we have a disagreement and then after we have sex, he thinks everything is all right and settled? Do you understand those deep needs of a man and why he functions like he does? He may not even understand why sex is so important to him either.

This book seeks to help you understand what motivates your mate so you can better understand him / her and therefore respond in appropriate ways. Also, this may give you insight as to why you are motivated to do what you do. With understanding comes the potential for change, as well as the enrichment of your relationship. Without understanding you will continue to do the same old thing and be frustrated in your relationship. Will you choose continual frustration or will you decide to pursue enrichment?

As you read this book you will find yourself saying "my partner needs to read this, because now I understand why I feel or act that way. I just haven't been able to articulate the importance of my needs clearly before. I want them to understand me better." The more we understand our own needs and how they fulfill us when they are met, the easier it is to understand the needs of our mate and, therefore, to value them.

The title I've chosen for this book is "The Dynamics of Communication and Sex. " The word Dynamic means *"Change producing force: the forces that tend to produce activity and change in any situation or sphere of existence"*. The content of this book helps you focus your understanding on the dynamics of sex and communication in your relationship.

After one of my sessions in reworking this manuscript I was taking a trip with my wife, and I said, "I wish we had a book like this available when we first got married, for it would have given us a better understanding of each other and helped us avoid a lot of mistakes." It is my desire that this book can help you avoid common pitfalls and deepen your relationship. Enjoy the journey!

Many relationships are frustrated because they don't understand the other persons' deepest need in their life, so I sought to make this a simple and interesting book.

**Kindle Books:** http://www.amazon.com/dp/B0072BVUJU
**Also in print:** http://www.amazon.com/What-Tone-Your-Communication-Relationship/dp/1492226319/

### Getting to Know You. Questions to help prepare for marriage.

This is a book of more than 300 questions that help you focus on many different areas important for a good relationship. It gives you the tough questions you need to ask yourself and the other person. One of the problems people have is that they don't spend enough time getting to know what each other thinks about their beliefs and views of life. The more surprises you uncover before marriage and talk out ahead of time, the stronger your marriage can be.

**This book** is one that parents will want to get for their teen or young adult children to help them understand some of the important issues of the makeup of a good relationship.

**This book** is designed to direct your thinking process for getting to know that special person. Do you really know the person that you are thinking of marrying? Do you know the kind of tough questions you need to ask?

**This book** of questions will assist you in your quest to gain understanding of that person who may become your life partner in marriage.

**This book** is made up of comments, observations and questions to guide you in your process of thinking realistically as you seek to get to know another person.

**This book** asks both the easy and difficult questions that help you reveal yourself to that special person and assist them in disclosing who they really are.

**This book** is not only important for those not yet married, but it can be of value for those who are already married.

**This book** is a wealth of common-sense questions that can help you avoid conflict in the years ahead.

**This book** offers several practical and informative helps in the supplemental section for those who are getting married, as well as for the newly married. Topics include understanding the other's world view, date night, setting goals, celebrating holidays, how to do a marriage tune up, and considerations for those who cohabitate. Added to the revised version is an article I wrote entitled "**Are you Entering Marriage as an Adult or a Child?**"

**Kindle Books: ASIN: B003VTZW71**

## Looking at Issues of Death and Suffering from a Christian Perspective

This book was born out of the tragedy of loss. It is not when life is easy that we learn those difficult lessons that make us think deeper, and drives us to higher levels of understanding. The result is that this kind of process compels us to move into greater levels of maturity. We don't enjoy those hardships of life, but if we are able to step back and consider the path we have traveled, we will observe important lessons we have learned. It may not be obvious if we only look at them from a human perspective, but when we see our tragedies, hardships, losses and pain from a divine perspective then some of life's difficulties begin to make more sense and we can cooperate more with God's purposes.

This book came as a result of me looking for answers to some of those questions that burn in our heart and mind when a young person dies. For me it was the death of my niece, Debbie. This book started as just a list. Later I taught it in our midweek services at the church. Eventually I taught a class in our Church on grief, and I got more serious in fleshing out the paper into a book. As I worked on the book, the direction broadened. I not only focused on why tragedy happens, but also on important considerations we must explore as we face any kind of suffering. What we learn in dealing with an untimely death often applies to other difficult situations in life as well.

An untimely death can come in many forms. Some seek escape from unpleasant situations in life by committing suicide, some die of health problems and complications. Others die in unfortunate accidents, and some are murdered. These aren't the only things that bring difficult questions into our life, or cause us to question God. People experience death of relationships through divorce, or death of their childhood through abuse and rape, and there are also deaths of dreams, such as losing a home in a foreclosure, losing a long-held job, or not being able to continue or finish college.

It is easy to see life from our own perspective, but suffering from loss also is an invitation by God to explore our life from His perspective. We will look at various facets of suffering and the kinds of questions that come to our mind for which we are seeking answers. This is a time we do much self examination about how we failed in some way. We seek to understand life, and to understand God and how he relates to us in such times.

As I wrote this book I felt that each section had to have some personal inquiry questions to help make that section more pointed. Not every section will apply to you, but the ones that do should be investigated in more depth, and that is the purpose of the questions.

This book deals with this topic of grief, loss, tragedy and suffering from a biblical and Christian perspective. It is not meant to be an exhaustive study, but something that is helpful for those who are facing these difficulties and wondering how to answer those questions that bombard their mind and keep them from having peace.

As I have shared this book I've come to realize that it is not a book for people when their emotions are still raw from their pain of loss. If you are having a hard time dealing with the loss of a loved one then I would recommend reading it at least six months after your loss. I've sought to address issues I've heard people talk about as they grieve their loss. I hope this helps with answers to the questions that have been plaguing your heart and mind. Sometimes we get so confused and we need someone to spark our thinking in a new direction.

Kindle Book: B006SJKSPO

# How Fast? How Far? How Big?

*Fun Facts for Kids about Speed, Distance and Size in Our Solar System and Universe. Trivia to Amaze Your Friends*

Often in science facts are taught but children have a hard time relating to such facts. In this book I seek to explain in understandable ways such things as the speed of light and size of stars and the distance between the sun and planets. Take a daring trip to the nearest star and jump into the center of the earth and sun. Making discovery fun is what this book is about.

http://www.amazon.com/dp/B00GI0SMLA

**Check out the Author Page:**
http://www.amazon.com/James-Olah/e/B005WLXP5O

# About the Author

James Olah, born in Muskegon, Michigan, has been a pastor for over 39 years. The focus of his teaching has always focused on helping people to experience life with higher goals and purpose. This book contains many of the papers he put together to help people grow in their faith over the years.

He and his first wife Nancy met while attending the same college in Grand Rapids, Michigan and they were married for 43 years. They have two grown children and five grandchildren. In February of 2012 Jim's wife died of cancer. He has dedicated a chapter of his book "Looking at the Issues of Death and Suffering from a Christian Perspective." to his wife that describes how he used the teachings of the book to help them go through this difficult time.

His interests have led him into many enriching experiences. He has been on the founding board of a graduate school (Moody Theological Seminary) in Detroit, Michigan and Yangon, Myanmar (Burma). He has contributed to a bimonthly magazine in India for eight years, written articles for local newspapers as well as many instruction papers for the people of his church.

Other experiences include his involvement in radio broadcasting for the oldest church owned radio station in the world, has been a co-host for a weekly cable Television broadcast, Eye Opener in Port Huron, Michigan, and on the broadcast television program called "Ask the Pastor". He was in the 1991-1992 edition of Who's Who in Religion. He volunteered in his local Alternative Education School for nine years with at-risk high school students and also volunteers as a hospice chaplain for 15 months and after retirement served as a staff chaplain for Hospice Advantage.

This book is one of two that deals with the aspects of the basic Christian faith. Early on in ministry he was involved in teaching the Coral Ridge Evangelism program and that helped him get a well grounded understanding of salvation as well as recognizing the need to disciple young Christians. "Town of Salvation" focuses on a clear explanation of salvation and how Christianity is unique among religions in how one is saved. This book is different than many in what it addresses about Christian growth. It is my desire that "Helps for Young Christians" will offer ideas and direction for those wanting to take their faith seriously. This book focuses on issues in a different way than most and issues that are imperative to helping the Christian stay on track for the Lord. I trust that it will be a well spring of information to help you in your journey.

24892590R670067

Made in the USA
Charleston, SC
10 December 2013